The Green Budget

The Green Party Council en-
dorses the publication of The
Green Budget. The views expressed are solely those of the
editors and not necessarily
those of the Green Party.

David Kemball-Cook

is spokesman for the Green Party on Treasury affairs. After taking a First Class BA (Hons) degree in Maths and Philosophy at New College, Oxford he did an MA in Operational Research at the University of Lancaster, then an MSc in Economics at Birkbeck College, London. He has worked on policy analysis with HM Customs and Excise, and has also done research in India (on rural electrification) and in Somalia (on famine relief) and now works as an economist at the London Business School and also teaches in further education (mathematics at Southwark College).

Chris Mattingly

is an engineer by primary qualifications (C.Eng, MICE, Enfield Tech) with a wide experience in industrial research, management, design and construction before retiring (at 48) to choose his own objectives. His wide experience, including twenty years living in communities, has given him an understanding of the way the political, personal and financial sides of our economy interact. In the Green Budget team he contributes not only through coordination and text revision, but also through original contributions in areas outside the range of conventional economics.

Mallen Baker

is the Green Party Speaker on Peace and Defence as well as a CoChair of the Green Party Council. He has been involved in political campaigning for most of his adult life, including work on peace and defence issues. He took part in a project to refurbish agricultural tools to send to Eritrea arising out of campaigns at the Molesworth Cruise Missile Base in Cambridgeshire, and went on to initiate a similar successful project in the South West. He has studied world politics with the Open University and has been an active participant in the Green Party's policy formulation process.

Janet Alty

- sub-editor and typesetter - has a degree in modern languages from Bryn Mawr College, USA and has learnt what she knows about economics by getting involved: she is currently Economic Policy Coordinator for the Green Party and was a CoChair of the Green Party Council and Convener of its Policy Committee 1987 - 1989.

The Green Budget

An Emergency Programme for the UK

edited by

David Kemball-Cook
Chris Mattingly
Mallen Baker

GREEN
PRINT

First published in 1991 by
Green Print
an imprint of The Merlin Press
10 Malden Road, London NW5 3HR

ISBN 1 85425 055 8

1 2 3 4 5 6 7 8 9 10 : : 99 98 97 96 95 94 93 92 91

Typeset by Janet Alty

Printed in England by Biddles Ltd., Guildford, Surrey
on recycled paper.

Contents

Foreword by Sara Parkin

Acknowledgements

This book follows from a Green Party 1990 Budget booklet which was written by members of this editorial team with Dean Buckner and Ben Schoendorff.

The editors take full responsibility for the final text.

We were unable to give many areas the treatment they deserve because of constraints of space and time. We trust that readers will give us their comments so that any future edition can be improved.

We gratefully acknowledge the following for their contributions: Victor Anderson, Deryck Artingstall, Adrian Atkinson, Sue Brown, Dean Buckner, Tony Cooper, Sara Parkin, Hugh Richards, David Simmons, John Valentine, Nigel Westaway.

The helpful comments and suggestions from the following are likewise gratefully acknowleged:
Sean Brady, David Chaplin, David Chapman, Tim Cooper, Roy Cuthbertson, Mercy Harmer, Michael Jacobs, Dr Tim Jenkins, Stephen Joseph, Brian Leslie, Rowland Morgan, John Morrissey, David Weston, Ian Wingrove.

Particular thanks are also due to Kathy Hammond of the Centre of Economic Forecasting at the London Business School for digging out statistics and creating graphs.

Foreword

Traveller, there is no path. Paths are made by walking.
(Australian Aboriginal saying)

In 1962 Rachel Carson launched the modern environmental movement with *Silent Spring*, her powerful book about dangers from chemicals to environmental and human health. Yet nearly 30 years later, despite mounting public concern and mountains of scientific warning, world pesticide use has multiplied 32-fold, and the rate of environmental degradation accelerates worldwide.

It seems astonishing that political leaders remain so out of step with this unique coalition of popular and scientfic concern. But if we look at the relationship between governments and those industries which have made the biggest contribution to planetary degradation, we might not be so surprised after all.

In all the economies of the developed world, it is energy-intensive, high polluting industries which make the largest contributions to GNP, the primary indicator of economic progress and (by association) successful government. In return, these industries receive the largest slice of government investment and patronage. If industry falters, so does government and vice versa, the circle of dependency is complete.

But the partners in this macabre dance of mutually assured economic destruction are bound to come crashing down eventually. A collapse of the environmental dance floor under their heavy tread will see to that.

This books casts a much needed beam of green hope that economic policies which favour low energy, low pollution strategies, could make it easier (and cheaper) for industry and ordinary people to lighten their step on the Earth. The dance, it is suggested, can be transformed from a dervish's whirl to a pastoral waltz.

The authors of this book are to be congratulated for turning the green vision of an ecologically sustainable society into a practical reality. They have conscientiously tackled the need to secure the position of the less well off in the short term, and carefully set radical change for all sectors of the economy in the context of a coherent medium term strategy.

The path is clearly signposted. Let us waste no more time and hurry down it.

Sara Parkin   Lyon, November 1990

INTRODUCTION

The price of progress

The 'eco' in economics, like the 'eco' in ecology, means house. Economics should therefore be about the proper management of the human demand on the global household. Instead it has become a calculus which deals only with things that are convenient to measure in money terms.

Over the past 40 years, the global economic product has nearly quintupled. Over the same period, world food output also grew at a record rate - the world's grain harvest is now two and a half times greater than it was in 1950. Technological developments have made it possible for human beings to visit the moon, and for words, images and financial transactions to circle the world in a matter of seconds. Ever increasing demand and consumption is regarded as the expression of a civilised society.

The cost in human and environmental terms of achieving this 'progress' is only just becoming clear. The indications are that the price that must be paid for 'human progress' may well be survival of humankind as a species on planet Earth.

Over the past 40 years, the world has lost nearly one fifth of its cropland topsoil, about a fifth of its tropical rainforests and tens of thousands of plant and animal species. Over-exploitation, sheer profligacy and pollution have reduced the world's fresh water supplies in some areas (the USSR and Poland, East and North Africa, the Middle East, India, China and parts of the US[31, 57] to critical levels. Since 1950 levels of atmospheric CO_2 have increased by 13%. At the Second World Climate Conference in November 1990, scientists reported their certainty that 'emissions resulting from human activities are substantially increasing the atmospheric concentration of the greenhouse gases ... resulting on average in an additional warming of the Earth's surface'.

Certain kinds of human activity have left their mark on the environment for many thousands of years - what is now the Sahara was once the breadbasket of the Roman Empire. The increasing numbers of people, plus the development of economies which are dependent on high inputs of energy and raw materials and the output of pollution, are now stretching not only regional but global life support systems to the limits.

A time for green economics?

Unfortunately politicians have not yet taken the message of these events to heart. They see the environment as basically peripheral to economic objectives. These objectives are fundamentally at odds with the need to maintain the life-support systems of the planet. They also conflict with respect for the dignity of peoples and the rights of other species.

The goals of conventional economic policy should be replaced. We propose three objectives:

• ecological sustainability
• equity across nations and across generations
• decentralisation of economic power to the lowest practical self-reliant communities.

There is a danger that ecological sustainability might be pursued as if it were achievable as a single goal. We believe that in order to preserve our biological life support systems we must also make fundamental changes in our value systems. The grim alternative is an increasingly inhospitable world exploited for the benefit of the few.

A green economy is one in which, whilst recognising the necessary environmental constraints, ensures that fundamental needs are met equitably throughout the world. This means that any production system must be based not only on minimum input, maximum retention and minimum output, but also on respect for the dignity of people.

Ecological sustainability

A sustainable economy is one which, broadly speaking, lives within the capacity of the planet to support life. It is capable of continuing itself into the indefinite future (as far as entropy and solar events will permit).[27]

Early ideas saw sustainability primarily in terms of safeguarding the limited supply of non-renewable resources like fossil fuels. However sustainability is more than that. Nature serves several vital functions for human society by providing non-renewable and renewable resources; a system for receiving and assimilating wastes; environmental services vital to life, such as air, water, soil, habitats, climatic stability, genetic diversity; and enjoyment, both material and spiritual.

We do not know how unsustainable our industrial economies have become, nor do we know if they can be transformed into a sustainable system. Science can only provide us with (albeit well-informed) guesses. We suggest that, at the very least, we have to seek:

• the preservation of remaining 'environmental capital'

• independence from the use of non-renewable resources

• consumption of renewable resources within sustainable yields

• cyclical production - ensuring the absorption of wastes without harm by the environment, the recovery and recycling of all valuable materials, and designing and building for long life

• the stabilising of population growth.

Equity within society:
across nations and across generations

Equity does not imply strict equality of wealth but rather the equality of rights to determine needs and to satisfy them. This puts an old ethical question into a new context.

The debt crisis has placed an impossible burden on the economies of many countries, so that governments of the South feel obliged to recycle hard cash to the rich countries of the North while their own society suffers deprivation beyond endurance. A greening of the world economy means not only changes in production, but also demands radical reforms to patterns of ownership, money systems and trading relationships.

A new ethical dimension is raised by the concept of equity across generations, stimulated by population growth and a degrading biosphere. Do not our descendants have the same right as ourselves to a decent environment? Even if there is no major breakdown of life support systems, it is still likely that future generations will have a worse environment than ours.

An economy is equitable if it:

• ensures that fundamental human needs are met

• recognises that within a local or national economy it is

essential to compensate the poorer sections of society against
any regressive taxation measures

• increases environmental capital to meet the needs of an
increasing population in the foreseeable future.

Decentralisation and self-reliant communities

Both economic and political power have increasingly been moved
away from individuals and communities to centralised governments. It is increasingly difficult for people either to understand
or to take responsibility for the implications of their actions. It
is an essential prerequisite of a green economy to restore both
economic and political power to the lowest practicable levels. The
biological system which support life are neither centralised nor
hierarchical, and any economic system which hopes to create
both equity and sustainability should seek to be likewise.

Central government cannot institute local self-reliance by de-
cree, but can remove the shackles which inhibit local economic
activity. A decentralised economy is therefore one which:

• gives increased responsibility to local communities for raising and spending revenue

• reduces reliance on centralised systems of energy, transport
and government

• enables people to meet their needs as far as possible from
their own local resources

• shields all participants in the economy from the damaging
effects of decisions over which they have no control.

The Green Budget strategy

The Green Budget does not reflect a new basis for economic
theory, but a concern to put economics in its proper place.
Economics must be subordinated to the interests of life on Earth.
The goals of policy should be changed accordingly. We must then
use all economic instruments available to try to achieve those
goals.

It is an illogical peculiarity of the UK economic cycle, which
no other country adopts, that the policies for revenue raising and
for spending are developed separately - the Budget with taxation
policy in March and the Autumn Statement in November. By
contrast we present a full Budget containing both the economic

instruments and the spending proposals.

The Green Budget strategy is threefold:

• to start to build an ecologically sustainable economy, via a new programme of environmental taxation. A proportion of the revenues would be recycled into the supply-side of the economy, to encourage conserving and sustainable technologies

• to attack the poverty trap with large increases in child benefit and the basic tax allowance. The medium term objective is an unconditional basic income of £35 per week for all citizens

• to begin decentralising the economy, with the poll tax and Uniform Business Rate to be replaced by locally-decided and locally-set taxation.

The green supply side

Much must be done urgently to regenerate the supply side of the economy to provide alternatives that are both more attractive and accessible. Investment in conservation and the cleaner alternatives will not only reduce directly the damage done to the environment, but will also make the taxation measures more effective as the supply side is improved. Without such investment the rates of carbon tax, for example, would be prohibitively high.

A supply side revolution is therefore needed, under which local industry, small industry and sustainable technologies generally will thrive. Our polices are intended to encourage this.

Dangerous and wasteful high-cost short-life production (of which the arms industry is the most obvious example) must be transformed into benign and conserving forms. The energy sector must develop the potential for conservation and the use of renewable sources. Transport must be weaned off the addiction to the motor car, and planning should replace mobility with accessibility. The tragedy of our disappearing rural communities can be reversed by a sensible agricultural and housing policy. Industry at all levels can be encouraged to invest in recycling and pollution control technology. Lastly we must start to invest properly in human potential and skills.

Environmental taxation, inflation and the poor

Environmental taxes are taxes placed on inputs or outputs for environmental reasons. In this Budget we propose a range of heavy and increasing environmental taxation. However we do not thereby accept the view, put forward by some environmental economists, that a value can be put on the environment and that this is a prequisite for environmental taxation.

To apply high environmental taxation is to increase taxes on expenditure. The criticisms are often made that this kind of policy is inflationary and regressive.

The objection that environmental taxes are inflationary is misplaced. The key point about environmental taxation is that it offers incentives to change to ways of living which do not bear this tax. If companies and individuals changed behaviour as ecological sustainability and equity require, for instance by conserving energy and generating electricity from renewable sources, then there would be no long term inflationary effect. This is why it is crucial to distinguish the short term (in which behaviour is assumed unchanged) from the medium and long term impacts.

The charge that environmental taxation is regressive is true up to a point. The effect on low income households is therefore considered and policy adapted accordingly. Revenues from environmental taxation are 'recycled' under our proposals. Part would be used for compensation for those on low incomes and part for regenerating the supply side of the economy (see above). A high proportion is made available in the form of increased tax allowances, increased child benefit, and grants specifically directed at the needs of the least well off.

For instance, it is argued by poverty campaigners[36, 54] that increased benefit payments to the 'fuel-poor' alone would not be sufficient to compensate for an increase in energy price. People who are fuel-poor are still very likely to respond to higher prices with less consumption, possibly at the risk of hypothermia. The campaigners argue that there should therefore be a nationwide programme of home insulation and other measures directed specifically at those most in need. We agree and support this proposal (see *Energy*).

In the case of transport we propose a large increase in petrol duty. This is (as with any indirect tax increase) a regressive measure which will badly affect those people on low incomes who are dependent on the motor car.

With progressively higher costs of motoring, poorer people would find that regular driving was the luxury of the rich. The poorest tenth would find a 70p rise in duty took 2% of their gross incomes (assuming no change in consumption), whereas the richest tenth would lose less than 0.7%. Effects of this sort in the short term are highly regrettable but unavoidable if the aim is to restrict the number of vehicles on the road. However most of the tax increase would fall on the middle income and wealthier households, since the poorest are even at present rarely car owners. There should be much better public transport provision in both urban and rural areas.

Limits and constraints

The Green Budget is a self-financing package of emergency measures that can be taken at once by a British government. Policies for the medium term are also put forward in each policy area.

This Budget is just a start on a long and painful journey for the British economy. The policies advocated will certainly not bring about sustainability, equity and decentralisation on their own. Just as taxation and investment must be linked into a coherent policy package, so these economic policies form only part of the package of changes necessary to achieve a green society.

Any government in today's world is extremely constrained in what it can do, in the face of the international money market, global corporations and multinational institutions like the European Community. However we have to start with those institutions and levers of power that are available in a democratic society, and trust that enough can be done in time.

1

Objectives, Targets and Indicators

The conventional objectives of economic policy

With the recognition that ecological sustainability is severely threatened, a new urgency has entered the debate about alternative goals and indicators. No society should put the future at risk. This requires a radical revision of conventional objectives.

Conventional economic policy relies very heavily on measuring by numbers. Every Chancellor's Budget speech includes statistics on the current state of the economy. Certain of these statistics have become known as 'economic indicators' and are used as the normal criterion or yardstick against which economic progress is measured.

When we are discussing economics and progress, it is essential that we should all agree what are the most important factors. In choosing which indicators to measure and pay attention to, we are choosing our priorities. We are stating what we value and what we don't value.

Those indicators which are regarded as most important in conventional economics are:

• **economic growth**, which is measured by increase in the Gross Domestic Product (GDP) or the Gross National Product (GNP).

• **inflation**, which is measured by increase in the retail price index.

• **balance of payments**, or current account, which means the net income of the UK from trade and interest payments etc. A negative current balance means the UK is going into debt to other trading nations.

• **unemployment**, which is measured as a percentage of the workforce.

The economic debate over the last 40 years, stated in simple terms, has been about how to increase economic growth and decrease unemployment without creating inflation or letting the balance of payments get out of hand. The last three indicators each measure something of importance and concern. However economic growth, despite being regarded as a prime objective, has the least relevance to reality. It measures nothing except the total of activity, regardless of what the activity is, or whether it contributes to health or wealth.

From our perspective, the key issues are the ecological sustainability of the economy and the level of human wellbeing, and there is no single indicator which can adequately measure those. We therefore propose to remove economic growth from its predominance and to replace it with targets for a battery of social and environmental indicators. Policy has then to be directed to achieving those targets.

Problems with inflation and unemployment

High inflation is clearly a threat to the stability of any society, as well as badly affecting those on fixed incomes. However it is foolish and simplistic to lump all price increases together as inflationary, without any judgment as to the function of the goods and their role in society. Yet this is what is done by the establishment parties and most economic commentators (see *Introduction*).

Unemployment too is clearly of some relevance as an indicator of social stress and the waste of human resources. But it is incorrect both to assume that only work done in formal employment has economic value, and to regard paid employment as the only work that is useful and satisfying. Equally, employment in the formal economy is a source of considerable stress to many people. We propose measures to liberate both work and people from the inflexibilities and unfairness of the present system of employment (see *Informal economy* and *Direct taxation*).

Why economic growth?

Gross Domestic Product (GDP) is the total yearly value, measured in money, of all the production in the country. The Gross National Product (GNP) has a very similar definition to GDP, but includes income (such as profits and dividends) from property or investments which UK residents own overseas. It excludes similar income from foreigners' investments in this country. In the case of the UK there is very little difference between the GDP and GNP figures.

If GDP or GNP shows an increase from one year to the next, economic growth is said to have been achieved. It simply means that more money has been exchanged for goods or services rendered in the last year after allowing for price increases. If GDP falls in successive quarters, this is described as a recession.

Problems with GDP and GNP

GDP and GNP are used by politicians and economists as measures of the basic health of the economy, and therefore the standard of living enjoyed by the population. If there is economic growth, the conventional assumption is that our collective standard of living has increased, in material terms, and that we are all 'better off' than last year.

There are so many problems with using economic growth as an index of well-being in such an uncritical way, that the assumptions have only to be questioned to be refuted. Only collective inertia and vested interests, combined with the relative ease of measurement, keeps GDP in such prominent use.

GDP measures only monetarily valued human economic activity. It values neither 'gifts of Nature' nor unpaid work. It does not differentiate between activities that add to well-being and environmentally damaging activities. The problem is not just that the GDP figures tell only part of the whole story (and fail to measure the essential non-monetary supports to economic life) but that many of the activities it does record are themselves damaging to the positive parts.

Until quite recently industrial society could ignore both the damage being done to natural systems, and the degradation of large sections of human society. The scale of human activity was relatively small compared to the surrounding biosphere. However, it is now no longer possible to do so. The existing indicators fail to show this damage, which is 'off the screen' and out of bounds to most economists. The crucial constraint on any economic system is its ecological sustainability. What are now urgently required are indicators that can tell us how near our society is to ecological and social breakdown.

Possible adjustments to GDP

One approach to finding alternative indicators is to adjust GDP and GNP in various ways. For example, every time that the money value of wood is added into GDP, the value of forest lost (including the loss of its contribution to wildlife, regulation of the climate etc.) would be subtracted. Such a figure is clearly a better estimate of income that can be maintained indefinitely, as is also a figure which would allow for the renewal and repair of the capital stock.

A 'Really Net' National Product could be estimated by using a figure for 'environmental depreciation'. This possibility has been discussed many times by environmental economists[13] but there are significant problems. Firstly, it is impossible to make a valuation objectively. How many pounds of environmental capital have been lost with the extinction of a species, for example? How much is the ozone layer worth? Despite this impossibility, economists have frequently tried at great length to set such monetary values.[41] And secondly, such a calculation still misses the basic point. No revision of GDP can tell us how much of our present income is sustainable into the future, because the crucial things are not factored in.

The answer is not to give money values to all the relevant environmental factors, but simply to say that the environment and well-being deserve separate consideration and equal or greater weight in decision-making.

The need for targets
and the example of global warming

The 1990 report on global warming from the Intergovernmental Panel on Climate Change (IPCC)[26] estimated that 'principally the long-lived gases (CO_2, nitrous oxide, and the CFCs) would require immediate reduction of emissions from human activities of over 60% to stabilise their concentrations at today's levels; methane would require a 15-20% reduction'.

There is almost certainly no 'safe' rate of global temperature increase. Yet if there were, the Stockholm Environment Institute (SEI) recently estimated[51] that it should be no more than 0.1°C per decade, with a total increase of no more than 2°C above preindustrial levels (1.5°C above today).

Global warming is a complex issue, and to combat it success-fully will require unprecedented international cooperation. Nevertheless the urgency of the situation and the now widely accepted 'precautionary principle' demand action be taken immediately. Some 75% of total CO_2 comes from industrialised countries so their reduction must be sufficient to give leeway for poorer, lower emitting countries to improve their quality of life, and accomplish the necessary technological transfers to develop their own sustainable economies.

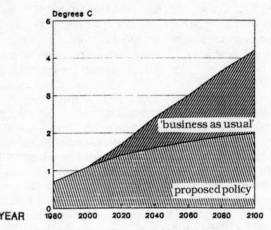

Figure 1.1 Temperature rise - 'business as usual' compared with reduction possible through proposed policy

We accept the 1990s as the turnaround decade; the main priorities are the prompt elimination of CFCs and the ozone-depleting chemicals, a rapid halt to deforestation and continuous world-wide reduction of net CO_2 emissions by 1-2% per year starting now (recommended by the Second World Climate Conference November 1990). Recognising the difficulty of setting exact targets and the possibility that more stringent reductions may be necessary, we propose an initial target for the UK of an average 30% cut in emissions by 2005 (from 1990 levels) of all greenhouse gases. The targets would differ according to the gas, with 30% being the level for CO_2. Gases such as methane with higher greenhouse potential would face a higher targetted reduc tion. After the year 2005, cuts in emissions may need to be more drastic, perhaps up to the 60% suggested by the IPCC.

The policies set out in this Budget, if continued by determined action over the next decade, have a good probability of meeting these targetted reductions for the UK. If they were followed by all the industrialised CO_2-emitting countries they would be able to provide the entire cut in CO_2 emission counselled by the climate scientists.

However, the links between policies, emissions and climate cannot be certain. Targets must be set for emissions of the principal greenhouse gases, and policies set to meet those targets. The uncertainty factor must be dealt with by constant monitoring and setting of appropriate indicators. Both policies and targets may need adjustment after comparison of actual and target emissions and assessment of the climatic effect, using an annual carbon audit, for example.

Alternative indicators

Many indicators of human well-being are already measured, like infant mortality, infection rates, literacy, and homelessness. Environmental indicators are also measured, such as carbon dioxide emissions, pollution of various kinds in air, soil and water, and loss of rural land in square miles per year.

Abandoning the search for an accurate Net National Product would mean replacing GDP and GNP as the primary economic policy objective, and using instead a whole set of indicators agreed to show true human and environmental well-being. This would represent an enormous shift in economic attitudes. This step, particularly if taken up by the seven major industrialised nations, would do more than anything else to shift definitions of economic progress away from growth measured in strict cash terms towards growth in ecological sustainability and human well-being, smoothing the way for more radical policy changes in the future.

For the critical national indicators targets must be set and fiscal policy has to be geared to meeting them. In this way we are beginning to submit 'UK plc' to a more accurate audit than in conventional economics. We also propose for the medium term that individual companies above a certain size be obliged to carry out environmental audits (as some large companies are now doing).

Budget Proposals

• Economic growth would be replaced by sustainability as an aim of economic policy.

• A set of key environmental and social indicators will be published and highlighted alongside existing economic indicators.

• A Medium Term Environmental Strategy will be announced, giving target figures for specific years for indicators such as carbon dioxide emissions, energy intensity and rainfall acidity

• A system for an annual carbon audit to be set up.

Medium Term proposals

• At the 1992 UN Conference on Environment and Development in Brazil, the UK will press for the promotion of a set of key environmental indicators and the setting of global targets.

• The structure of UK government will be reorganised so that targets for environmental and social indicators are brought into the centre of decision-making This will involve radical changes in the workings of the Treasury.

• The regular monitoring and updating of the Medium Term Environmental Strategy will become increasingly central to UK economic policy.

• As part of a general strategy of decentralisation, indicators will increasingly be compiled on a local basis in consultation with local communities.

• As more data become available the list of key indicators will be expanded.

2

Direct Taxation and Basic Income

Direct taxation is levied directly on citizens. It has historically been placed either on income or wealth. Income tax was introduced as a temporary measure to pay for the Crimean War, and proved so convenient that it now raises over a quarter of public revenue. It is still a very reliable way of raising money because many people cannot evade it since it is deducted at source from their wages or salary.

In conventional economics labour has been treated as a scarce factor of production. The process of economic growth has promoted substitution of labour by capital-intensive machinery and technology, and hence by fossil fuel energy and irreplaceable resources. When fossil fuels and resources appeared abundant and the environment posed no constraints, this made economic sense. Now it does not - the true scarce factors of production are land, resources, fossil fuel energy and the capacity of biospheric support systems - and labour is abundant (and becoming increasingly so worldwide). It is therefore sound economics to move the burden of taxation from human effort and human-made capital onto those scarce factors of production, land, energy and resources.

Two major reforms to the system are necessary, and can be initiated in the Budget:

• to change the way the tax and benefit systems interact to produce what are known as the poverty and employment traps. These changes will also encourage a liberating attitude to work, and will help us to move towards the kind of society we will need in the next century.

• to change the effect of the tax system on housing and land. Through mortgage tax relief home-ownership has been subsidised, making it more difficult for poorer people to find housing.

Also the way land is treated as an investment for profit has meant that speculation is rewarded, and control of land tends to pass away from immediate occupiers into the hands of financial institutions

Taxation and the changing economy

During the 1970s and early '80s it became increasingly clear that while an advanced industrial economy can generate enormous material wealth, it cannot distribute it in an equitable fashion with similar ease. Nor can it guarantee full-time paid work to all who want it. Still less can it guarantee meaningful and satisfying work. Least of all is such work available where people want to live.

Economic strategy since 1945 has been to 'buy off' the social costs associated with economic growth with an expansion of public spending, particularly on the welfare state. So long as the overall cake was growing, the ingredients or the quality of the cooking did not seem to matter.

To regard economic growth as the solution to all problems is now an increasingly implausible position to take. To make matters worse, the cuts made in recent years in the key sectors of energy, transport, education and training will be showing increasing effect, and a descent into a deeply divided and impoverished society will be hard to avoid.

Conventional thinking about the future has assumed both continued dependence on a welfare state for large numbers of people and reliance on full-time paid employment to provide the income for the majority of households.

The first assumption is undesirable. The second is unrealistic, if there is less and less full-time work available.

However, diminishing opportunities for full-time employment can be used creatively. Part of the solution to our economic and environmental problems may lie in greater reliance on the informal economy (see *The informal economy*).

Likewise, if people are able to satisfy more of their needs in or near their homes without having to travel far to work, then not only will they live better quality lives, but also fewer resources will be used and less strain put on the environment. The tax and benefit system can be changed to accommodate and encourage this development, principally through a basic income scheme (see below).

Income tax collected through the Pay As You Earn (PAYE) system has worked reasonably well and will clearly remain an important part of the system. However the tax will be harder to collect when the majority of people work casually or informally without a formal employer/employee relationship.

Benefits and the poverty trap

The welfare state was intended to be only a safety net for a small minority. The number of recipients of income support is now approaching two million. The level of benefit is widely perceived to be barely enough to live on. Although benefits are uprated each November for inflation, we propose an additional increase in this Budget of 5% as part-compensation for the increases in taxation we propose (see *Environmental taxation*).

The 1988 Fowler changes in income support (which affected young people and the homeless) and the replacement of special needs payments by loans were particularly miserly and cynical acts. They saved only a small amount of money but severely affected many people on the poverty line, and we would rescind them.

The means-tested benefit system has direct disadvantages in the way people are treated and the bureaucracy needed to administer it. The way it combines with the tax system has even more serious consequences. These are known as the poverty trap and the unemployment trap.

In the poverty trap a large number of people in work can get little extra to take home from a pay rise. An increase in income for low earners is not only subject to tax but also leads to a reduction of means-tested benefit. The bizarre situation arises of families on low income being in receipt of benefit (family credit), but also paying tax and facing a marginal tax rate of nearly 100%. In many cases a pay rise means an actual reduction in disposable income.

The unemployment trap arises from the fact that unemployment benefit and income support are available only to the completely unemployed. Many unemployed people have little or nothing to gain financially by seeking a job.

Reforms to the system are long overdue. The traps arise from the multiplicity of benefits that are means-tested. The only significant non means-tested benefit is child benefit, whose value has been frozen since 1987 (except for the largely cosmetic uprating for the first child in 1990).

We propose an immediate 50% increase in child benefit. This is the most effective measure that can be taken to help families on low income to climb out of poverty. It is also particularly helpful to women, because it is paid directly to the mother. In the longer term the best approach to the poverty trap is the introduction of a basic income payable to adults and children alike.

National Insurance contributions

The first reform to make is both obvious and overdue. National Insurance (NI) contributions are only paid on the first £350 per week of earnings. This means that the marginal rate of tax falls as incomes pass this threshold. NI is now an illogical and regressive adjunct to income tax. Most suggestions for reform retain the fiction that the contributions are different from income tax, but abolish the upper earnings limit. We prefer the more consistent alternative of abolishing NI altogether. Employees' contributions are then consolidated into the basic rate of income tax. This could be done in the first year.

The new basic rate would therefore be 34p in the pound. To this would be added the temporary 6p local income tax supplement needed in the first year to pay for the abolition of the poll tax (see *Local government*).

Employers' NI contributions are simply a payroll tax, another tax on labour. This would probably have to be retained for for the first year (but renamed a payroll tax for the sake of honesty). In following years it could be abolished, and the equivalent revenue obtained from a reform of company taxation.

Personal allowances

The best way of helping to relieve the poverty trap in the short term is a substantial increase in the basic personal allowances. We propose to increase them by 50%.

With the current system of allowances, high earners benefit disproportionately from an increase in allowances. The present single allowance of £3,005 is worth £751 to the basic rate payer, but worth £1,202 to the higher rate payer. We propose a zero rate income tax system where allowances only provide relief at the basic rate. This means that higher rate payers pay tax at a given threshold, rather than at a given amount of taxable income.

More progressive taxation

In 1988 the Chancellor reduced the top rate of income tax from 60% to 40%, saying that the new low rates would encourage (rich) people to work harder and bring in more revenue. But low rates might equally discourage people from working harder, as they would not need such a high gross income to obtain the same net income as before. Certainly the richer section of society has been paying more as a proportion of total revenue in recent years, but that is more probably the wealthy are getting richer.

Before 1979 the highest rate of tax was 83%. That was high enough to ensure a good deal of tax evasion. In our view 40% is too low as a highest marginal rate, and 80% too high. We propose a top rate of 52%, coming in at a gross annual income of £30,000. We also propose a new intermediate rate of 44% payable when £24,000 income is reached, a little lower than the current threshold for the higher rate. These figures *include* the 9% NI contribution. Those whose weekly pay is over £350 will be paying more than their previous overall payment. Between 8% and 10% of tax payers would then be paying tax at the intermediate rate.

For the basic rate of income tax we propose a cut of 1p in the pound, from 34p (the present 25p plus the 9p for NI contributions) to 33p. This again will have the effect of lessening the poverty trap.

We estimate that the overall impact of these changes will be a reduction in direct tax revenue of about £1.9bn, taking into account the loss of approximately £13bn from employees' National Insurance contributions. There is a large reduction of revenue resulting from raising the tax threshold by one half (perhaps a loss in annual revenue of £9bn if implemented on its own), but this is mostly compensated for by the more progressive rates of income tax and the extension of the 9% former NI tax to all higher income bands.

As an additional measure to promote saving in the local economy we propose that interest on all deposits in the new community banks (see *Monetary policy*) be relieved of income tax.

A basic income scheme

A basic income (BI) is the fairest and most logical way of removing the poverty and employment traps. It also brings more general benefits to the greening of the economy. A basic income provides much greater freedom in people's choice of work, and a platform of support for individuals and families during the period of radical and painful changes that faces us. It can also underpin the re-education and re-training that will be necessary. The obstacle to implementation of a BI scheme is not primarily technical (as some claim), but the inertia of the system. The critical factor is political will.

The essential characteristic of a basic income is that it is not withdrawn as income rises, unlike current means-tested benefits. Payment is made to individuals or their guardians on the basis of citizenship, and not on criteria of income or unemployment (although there would be supplements for particular groups, see below). It can be operated as a 'convertible tax credit' (like current child benefit) which is paid as a tax-free benefit to those on low incomes, but for those on higher incomes it counts as a credit against tax.

If the BI is large enough to replace means-tested benefits then full integration of the tax and benefit systems is possible. Under this a single system replaces all benefits, tax allowances and tax reliefs. Every adult then faces the same net tax schedule, and there are no administrative distinctions between net beneficiaries and net taxpayers. A fully integrated system is difficult to achieve in practice, but partial integration with residual means-tested benefits could be implemented in a fairly short time.[40]

There has been considerable debate about what level of a basic income is desirable and also about what is practical. A full basic income would, let us say, be in the region of £60 per week (in 1990 terms) per adult, sufficient to cover basic needs and approximately equal to current income support plus housing benefit. In a household of two adults (able to work) and two children this would provide an unconditional weekly income of around £180. Such a level would permit full integration.

Objections are made that a full BI of at least the levels of current income support would be both impractical and erode the incentive to take employment. However a partial BI in the region of £25 to £35 per week (in 1990 terms) would in our view overcome these objections. For single people able to work and willing to share housing costs it could be enough for basic needs. If a partial BI is combined with appropriate supplements to basic income for full-time carers and others, allowances for the disabled, tax discounts for low earners (the same for men and women), residual housing benefit and emergency benefit payments, it could largely replace income support, family credit and unemployment benefit.

Figures 2.1 & 2.2 illustrate the effects of a partial BI (based on the figures in Appendix 2 of [40]) by showing how disposable income increases with gross income, compared the present system (using 1985-86 incomes data). The poverty trap in the present tax/benefit system is shown clearly in the nearly flat slope of the graphs in both Figures for low levels of income. The considerable redistribution in favour of the poor is shown by the

Figure 2.1 and 2.2

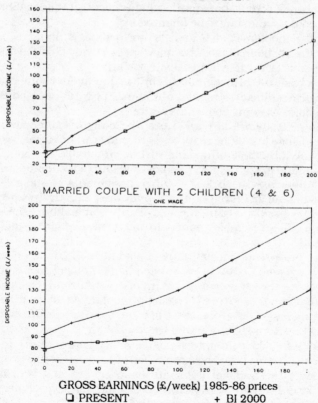

SINGLE NON-NOUSEHOLDER

MARRIED COUPLE WITH 2 CHILDREN (4 & 6)
ONE WAGE

GROSS EARNINGS (£/week) 1985-86 prices
❑ PRESENT   + BI 2000

amount by which a partial BI disposable income exceeds present levels for low incomes. The redistribution is achieved by more progressive taxation and the abolition of all or nearly all tax reliefs.

It would be possible to introduce a partial scheme in stages, gradually reducing the poverty trap and the numbers on means-tested benefit. The most logical method is to pay BI as a convertible tax credit through the tax system, like child benefit. For most taxpayers the impact would be as a progressive increase in their basic allowance.

The gross annual cost of a partial BI of £30 pw would be between £70bn and £75bn. However, between £25bn and £30bn of the sums currently spent on pensions, income support and other benefits would be saved, leaving a net cost of about £45bn. This could, for instance, be financed by:

- the abolition of all tax reliefs (worth about £15bn)
- the abolition of most tax allowances leaving only the first £20 per week tax free (worth about £20bn)
- a basic rate of income tax of 40p (yielding about £8bn extra)
- higher rates of income tax of 45p and 55p with our proposed thresholds (yielding about £2bn extra)

However, there is no need to meet the total cost of the scheme from income tax. Other sources of revenue can be earmarked, with the advantage of making BI less vulnerable to political dispute and manipulation. One possible source is our proposed site value tax (see below). Other possibilities are a given percentage of VAT receipts, the revenue from an extra 1p, 2p, or 3p on the basic rate of income tax, or any combination of these. BI would then resemble a national dividend rather than a welfare benefit.

We propose as our first target an adult BI of £35pw before 1995, implemented in stages. At each stage all other benefits are reduced by the value of the BI. Many of those currently claiming income support who could find employment would then find it in their interest to do so and cease to claim benefit. The numbers doing this would increase with the level of BI.

For a BI to be paid universally requires registers of all adult citizens. These should be maintained by local authorities, and linked to the national (integrated) income tax and benefits database. There is a possible role here for the poll tax machinery, which would otherwise be dismantled under our proposals. If this were used, local authorities could administer BI as agents of the government. During the transition BI could be paid only to those non-taxpayers who claimed it (although the value to most taxpayers would automatically be credited to them).

As BI reaches our first target level of £35pw (in 1990 terms) much of the apparatus of the welfare state will be supplanted. There will remain the need for residual payments for special needs and housing costs, as well as supplements for pensioners, disabled people, single parents and others. Unemployed people would be able to choose between remaining on income support or using their BI to reach economic independence.

The longer term effects of BI, alongside other measures and developments, would be far-reaching. The economy would be adjusting to different attitudes to work and the community learning different ways of helping those on low incomes.

Mortgage tax relief

Mortgage tax relief has a strange origin. Until the 1960s owner-occupiers were taxed for the 'rent' they enjoyed from living in their homes. To make their tax position equivalent to people renting homes, their mortgage interest payments were relieved of tax. However in 1963 this imputed rent was relieved of tax, but the mortgage relief remained. The result has been a continuing subsidy to owner-occupation.

In the 1980s house prices have inflated by far more than incomes or retail prices, and this tax subsidy was one of the reasons. This contributed to the consumption boom of the late 1980s and led to the near-disappearance of the private rented sector. It has also badly affected many rural communities, as many young residents have found themselves unable to afford to buy a house where they grew up.

The tax system can be used to get asset prices down to levels which reflect use value without a speculative element. We propose that mortgage tax relief should be restricted to the basic rate of income tax immediately. We would also limit relief to the first ten years of a mortgage, which would concentrate it to where it was most needed. This could be implemented in the following year.

Site value taxation

Society currently permits the private ownership of land and the appropriation of the economic rent. In effect, land is treated just like any capital asset such as buildings or machinery. It can be treated as a speculative investment, like a work of art, expected to maintain or increase its value in real terms.

The problems lie both in how land ownership is regarded and in how land use is decided. In sustainable tribal societies, the land is a sacred trust, held for the benefit of all, and not private property. We need to return to something like this way of perceiving land, and the taxation system can be used to help develop it. Land ownership can become more like the right to practise a kind of stewardship, and income can be restricted to the direct return available from its use.

Communal ownership of the land is the solution adopted by tribal societies, but it is not a practical measure in a highly urbanised and industrial society. Land nationalisation has been widely canvassed. This would merely replace private institutional ownership of land with state ownership.

In our view the best approach to the problem of land use is to use the planning and the tax systems together, within the context of a market economy modified and constrained by the state. It will not provide an instant solution, but represents the best set of options available. In order to preserve rural land from unwelcome development, much tighter planning controls are needed. In order to prevent land becoming an object of speculation or investment, taxation directed at the economic rent would be effective.

The ownership of land provides a stream of income, known as the economic rent, which is strictly surplus to the payments for labour and capital used on that land. The economic rent comes from exploitation of the mineral or other resources, the quality of the soil, or (with urban land) the surrounding community. The private appropriation of the economic rent by landowners makes land speculation lucrative and separates land ownership from those who work and live on it. To tax the economic rent of land (rural and urban) would begin to return land ownership to those using it directly.

Our Budget proposes for the medium term a tax on the site value of all land in residential or business use, levied either on the occupier or the owner. Such a tax has long been advocated by some economists (most recently by Muellbauer[35]). It is practised in many cities in other countries including the US and Australia and is widely recognised to yield real economic benefits. Its main effect is to economise on land use in urban areas, reducing land held idle and encouraging all land to be used to its fullest potential (within existing planning permission). It reduces the motive for land speculation and brings down land capital values, and house prices with them. A further benefit could be the revival of the private rented sector as existing properties are put to fuller use.

A site value tax on a UK-wide basis could be integrated with the national component of income tax for owners of residential land. Integration with income tax is important for small landowners on low earnings, because there would then be tax allowances available to offset the liability. For business land it could be used as a basis for reformed business rating.

In recent years consumption has grown strongly because people have felt wealthier as house prices rise. A general relative reduction in land and house prices as a result of these reforms will help to cool off the economy.

Bringing people out of the tax net

If, as argued above, there will be a significant reduction in the number of families with a member in formal full-time employment, there will be a need to reduce the dependence of the tax base on the PAYE system. Even under the current system, we believe on grounds of both social justice and cost-effectiveness that as many people on low earnings or in part-time working as possible should be brought out of the direct tax net.

The tax base of the future would be based much more on companies operating in the formal economy, expenditure on goods produced and traded, and land and property, rather than on individual incomes declared to the Inland Revenue.

Budget proposals

Direct taxation
• Increase in income tax personal allowances by 50%
• Conversion of income tax allowances to a tax credit system with a zero rate and income thresholds for all higher rates
• Consolidation of employees' NI contributions into income tax
• Cut in the basic rate of income tax by 1p, making a new basic rate of 33p
• Temporary local income tax/poll tax addition of 6p to basic rate (revenue not included here see *Local government*)
• Restriction of mortgage tax relief to the basic rate
• Intermediate rate of income tax of 44p at a threshold of £24,000 gross annual income
• Higher rate of 52p at a threshold of £30,000
• Interest on deposits in community banks to be relieved of income tax
• Employers' NI contributions to be obtained from a reform of company taxation
Impact : Loss of revenue (tax cut) £1.9bn

Welfare benefits
• Increase in child benefit by 50%   £2.2bn
• Increase in income support and pensions by 5% above inflation to compensate for indirect tax increases (£1.5bn)
• Reversal of 1988 changes in rules for income support affecting the young and homeless   £0.1bn
Impact: Cost £3.8bn

Medium term proposals

• Implementation of local income tax as a facility for local government revenue-raising (see *Local government*)

• Limiting mortgage tax relief to the first 10 years and to the basic rate of income tax

• Introduction before 1995 of a basic income with a target level of £35pw plus BI supplements and tax allowances on earned income

• Introduction of a site value tax on land, to be integrated with personal income tax for residential land

• Reform of company taxation

3

Environmental Taxation

All forms of life create waste. Human society is currently producing waste in a form and in amounts which are beyond the capacity of the natural systems of the biosphere to manage. This is pollution and is damaging the life-support systems of the Earth to such a degree that the future of human life is threatened. Environmental taxation is one of the mechanisms which can be used to bring about the changes in human activity necessary for our survival.

Environmental taxation is taxation applied to two distinct but interrelated environmental goals: the discouragement of pollution and the conservation of resources. All environmental taxation increases the costs of production in an attempt to reflect true environmental and social costs.

There are three general categories of environmental taxation:

• the first are **taxes on inputs** to the production process, either because their use in production releases pollutants, or because those inputs are irreplaceable raw materials.

• the second are **charges on outputs**, i.e. the waste products. Legal limits are set for discharges. Producers can then be charged per unit of legal discharge.

• the third is **consumption taxation**, paid directly on products as they are sold. This has not received as much attention as the first two (see *Indirect taxation*).

It is clear that environmental taxation is inadequate on its own. It is therefore vital to consider environmental taxation alongside other measures, in particular those which address technology and the supply side of production (see *Introduction*).

All environmental taxes lead to rises in the price of basic necessities like food, heating and transport. A criticism of environmental taxation in general therefore is that it is regressive, in other words it falls hardest on the poorest members of society. This is a serious objection, and measures to compensate or help the poorest in some way must be incorporated into any environmental policy package (see *Direct taxation*, also *Introduction*).

Costing the environment

The questions of whether and how the environment can be costed are outlined in detail in the Pearce Report.[41] This approach is seriously flawed. Most forms of environmental damage, especially generalised disruption such as global warming, do not lend themselves to being costed except in rough terms. In our view many of the methods used by cost-benefit analysis to value the environment are highly suspect, because they seek to dress up highly subjective processes in the clothes of scientific method. The rates at which environmental taxation is set cannot be chosen by exact science, but are operated in a pragmatic way in order to achieve desired effects. The effects of taxes and other measures should be continuously monitored, and adjusted to meet policy targets (see *Objectives*).

Taxes, charges or regulation?

Taxation or pollution charging are often thought of as alternatives to regulation as a way of achieving environmental goals. The important principle is that the amount of pollution produced should not be allowed to exceed the ability of the environment to absorb it. The problem with regulation alone is that there are no incentives to reduce emissions below the legal limits.

Any system which relies on regulation to set maximum limits is only as good as the knowledge on which they are based. It is therefore essential for quotas to be set according to the best available local knowledge (as already happens to some extent) rather than using generalised national statistics.

The arguments against pure reliance on taxation or charging are also persuasive. Taxation imposed at a national level will be incapable of variation to meet local circumstances. In some localities the ecological balance is more fragile than others, and effective pollution control should take account of this.

In some cases regulation is self-evidently more effective than taxation in achieving a given goal. It would be possible, for instance, to introduce a tax on non-returnable containers for beverages to encourage re-use and discourage waste. However it would be far simpler and more effective to legislate that all drinks be sold in standardised returnable bottles.

A similar argument applies to the use of ingredients or additives, such as chlorofluorocarbons (CFCs), which have known harmful effects and yet for which substitutes exist. The solution is to ban them, not tax them.

Environmental taxation and international trade

If one country introduces heavy environmental taxes on inputs unilaterally, then its goods will become more expensive relative to those from other countries. There would be a tendency to import more goods from countries less concerned about pollution and resources, effectively exporting environmental problems (usually to poorer nations) without solving them. The country would also find its domestic industry becoming uncompetitive in the global market.

The logical solution to this problem is to impose equivalent import duties on foreign goods that do not bear domestic environmental taxes. This will be a 'default' rate of tax, but importers who can prove that the resource content or pollution factor is lower will then pay a lower tax. Domestic industry can then be protected to some extent, but several difficulties remain:

• there would be conflict with EC legislation - unless of course the taxes and duties were imposed on a Community-wide basis

• there are practical difficulties in determining the import duties equivalent to a given range of environmental taxes

• the problem of increased uncompetitiveness would remain unless most trading partners can be persuaded to implement the same taxes. For a country with a huge balance of payments deficit, this is a serious issue

• there is an ethical problem associated with a government of the rich industrialised north raising revenue by taxing the countries of the poor south.

These issues highlight the importance of obtaining international agreements, and the difficulties surrounding unilateral introduction of major environmental taxation (see *Europe and world trade*).

Input taxation: carbon

Global warming represents the most serious potential threa
human survival after that of nuclear war (for discussion se
Objectives). Carbon taxes at national or global level have been
proposed as part of a strategy to reduce emissions of CO_2 and
other greenhouse gases and reverse the process of climate
change. The development of a common international framework
would make them much more effective than unilateral measures. Agreement at the 1992 Climate Conference in Brazil is
therefore crucial.

In September 1990 the European Commission began consideration of a common framework for the imposition of taxes on
emissions from fossil fuels based on their potential for contrib-
uting to the greenhouse effect. Countries such as Sweden are
leading the way in declaring their plans for the adoption of a
carbon tax. There is no further excuse for inaction, and any
budget presented in the UK will be completely inadequate
without such measures. The difficulties of obtaining international consensus cannot be allowed to stand in the way.

The primary purpose of a tax on CO_2 production is to
encourage the use of low carbon or no carbon fuels, the production of electricity from renewable sources, and energy conservation. A carbon tax would differ from a simple energy tax in being
targetted at the carbon content of any fuel at point of production.
Different fuels would be taxed at different rates to reflect this.

Estimates made by Scott Barrett of the London Business
School suggest that such taxes could be very effective in changing patterns of use over ten years. Barrett estimated (using Department of Energy estimates of elasticities of demand for
energy) that the tax rates required to reduce CO_2 emissions by
20% in 10 years would be gas 14%, oil 19%, and coal 24%.[5]

Estimates made by other economists differ wildly according
to the models used and the assumptions made, but most
estimates of effective rates are much higher than Barrett's. For
instance the International Energy Agency estimated rates would
have to be 100% for coal and 50% for oil (for Europe) merely to
stabilise growth of production of greenhouse gases by 2005.
Terry Barker estimated that to achieve targets by 2005, rates of
tax would have to rise progressively to reach a massive 374% for
coal, 327% for oil and 141% for gas.[4]

One of the reasons why economists obtain such large per-

...rgy demand responds very sluggishly to ...This is why it is vital to accompany such ...measures.

...ate measure which would be encouraged ...uld be the substitution of natural gas for ...duction in the short term before the use of renewable .... becomes more widespread. This would reduce the CO_2 by 40% and could be done fairly quickly because existing coal-fired plant can readily be converted to burn gas.

The carbon tax would be a substantial source of revenue. The Institute for Fiscal Studies estimated annual revenue from a 10% tax at about £3bn, using Barrett's estimates and assuming current patterns of energy spending.[42] Revenue should fall as the tax achieves its purpose.

Carbon taxation must of course be seen within a framework of a complete package of energy policy, comprising large pro-grammes of investment into renewable and non-polluting sources of energy, into energy conservation and efficiency, compensation measures for the fuel poor and global negotiations (see *Energy*).

We propose rates of taxation for the first year, somewhat lower than Barrett's short term figures, of 10% for coal, 8% for oil and 6% for gas. The rates should be increased progressively and predictably over the next ten years. We estimate that revenue in the first year would be just under £2bn (after allowing for the changes in consumption). In the medium and long term consumption of coal and oil in particular can be expected to fall quite substantially.

Input taxation: nitrogen

There is great concern about nitrates in the water supply. The amount of chemical nitrogen fertiliser used in farming has made the issue particularly acute in East Anglia and other areas where arable farming is predominant.

Historically the pattern of agriculture has always been mixed animal and arable farming, so that wastes become useful sources of nutrient. Problems arise whenever the two are separated geographically. The clear solution to the problems of unwanted agricultural wastes is to foster a general return to mixed farming, and from that to organic agriculture.

One of the mechanisms available is to impose taxes on chemical fertilisers, rendering mixed farming more economic.

The most feasible first option is a tax on nitrogen-based fertilisers. However such a tax would have to be high to have appreciable effects on farmers' use of fertiliser (Table 3.1). Even if heavily taxed, fertiliser remains cheap compared to the increases in yield it offers in the short term. The average farmer would be inclined to use almost as much fertiliser as before. The resulting impact on nitrogen concentration will therefore be limited.

Table 3.1: Estimated effects of a nitrogen tax

Tax rate	Revenue collected (£m)	Change in total farm output (£m)	Reduction in farm profits (£m)	Change in nitrate concentration (%)
5%	15.2	-	15.5	- 0.7
10%	31.4	- 17.7	31.1	- 1.4
20%	65.8	- 37.4	62.5	- 2.6
40%	142.0	- 82.3	126.3	- 5.0

Source ICI/London School of Economics

If government expenditure is required for measures such as additional water purification and appropriate grants to farmers it is only fair that the polluters bear at least some of the cost. (For our proposals on income support for farmers see *Agriculture*.) We propose a nitrogen tax of 40%, with a target of reducing nitrate concentration by 5%.

Input taxation: resource taxes

In the longer term it is a logical development of input taxation to institute a range of input taxes on all raw materials. Such taxes would reflect their relative scarcity, economic value, and (possibly) the environmental disruption caused by their extraction. At present the UK has a duty on hydrocarbon oils, which performs this role. The proposed carbon tax would supplement this for oil, and act as a resource tax for coal. However there is a strong case for taxing metals, irreplaceable minerals and hardwoods.

The taxes would have to be highly differentiated in both level and operation according to the implications of the use of the particular material. They would, for the most part, operate like existing excise duties, and should, in the case of home materials, be levied at the stage closest to the point of extraction. For imported raw materials they could be levied on import.

Resource taxes are clearly best introduced within an international or EC framework, for the reasons outlined above concerning international competitiveness. However we propose that the UK should implement them on a unilateral basis pending international agreements. Introduction would have to be in stages, with likely candidates for a first phase being tropical hardwoods and fossil fuels.

Output taxation: pollution charges

Is there a role for charging for the pollution which is emitted within legally agreed limits? Output taxation in the form of pollution charges is the subject of some controversy among environmentalists. It is felt that if a given level of pollution is damaging then it should be stopped, not taxed.

Two arguments are made in favour of pollution charges being more effective than regulation:

• a charge is paid on all units of pollution, thereby providing a constant incentive to develop cleaner technology. With direct regulation it is enough to comply with the minimum legal requirement.

• within a given range of technologies, the cleanest will tend to become adopted. This provides an incentive to get the greatest possible production while keeping emissions within the legal limits.

Pollution charges follow from the Polluter Pays Principle, which was first laid down by the Organisation for Economic Cooperation and Development (OECD).[39] The danger with this concept is that it can too easily turn into one whereby he who can pay can pollute. Pollution charges are also subject to the defect that they rely on reasonably accurate and honest measurement of discharges, and tend to require considerable amount of policing. Many pollutants are dangerous below the sensitivity of current measuring equipment.

More controversial is the idea of marketable pollution licences or permits, which may be bought and sold between producers. The licences are issued or sold by government within an overall limit for the area in question. A firm which invests in cleaner technology may then sell its unwanted quota to other producers.

In theory tradeable licences provide an incentive for achieving the most efficient method of production with a limited quantity of pollution. Such a system permits new producers with much cleaner technology to establish themselves and compete with the more established and dirtier companies, forcing them either to go out of business or to adopt the new technology. The idea has been tried in the U.S.A., and some success in controlling air pollution is claimed.[5]

Tradeable permits for CO_2 production have also been proposed for the international arena, where initial licences might be issued (for instance) on the basis of population. Northern nations would then have to cut emissions quite drastically, unless they purchased permits from Southern nations where CO_2 production per head is much lower. Clearly this would provide a means of making resources available to poorer countries for investment in cleaner technology, and must be examined in this light.

In conclusion, although it is dangerous and complacent to rely on pollution charges to achieve environmental goals, there could be a proper role for them within an overall context of national and local regulation which sets realistic and safe limits to emissions. We propose a system of charging at levels which would ultimately have a real impact on behaviour, and would therefore be likely to have a significant effect on prices.

Transport taxation

Transport policy and energy policy together present the most urgent challenges for a green economic strategy. Heavy traffic contributes massively to both global and local pollution, making our cities dirty and noisy, and threatening the health of all who come into contact with it. In 1987, UK road vehicles produced 98m tonnes of carbon dioxide (16% of total emissions), 1m tonnes of nitrogen oxides (45% of the total) and over 4m tonnes of carbon monoxide (85% of the total).[10]

Fuel pricing and vehicle ownership

The principle of environmental taxation indicates higher taxation of the motor car and the lorry. The question is whether it should fall on the use of vehicles (via petrol and DERV duty) or on their possession (via vehicle excise duty).

Vehicle Excise Duty (VED) is a tax on car ownership. Some have advocated that it be increased, and/or that it be differentiated by engine size to penalise larger cars. Measures to make car ownership prohibitively expensive would be simple-minded and counter-productive. They would discriminate against those who depend on the car, such as those living in rural areas, pensioners, some families with small children, and people with disabilities, and for whom no immediate alternative exists. It would be a highly regressive measure which would penalise those on low incomes who are dependent on cars.

It is a basic principle of environmental taxation that such taxes be placed at the margin. Roughly speaking, this means that pollution charges should increase in proportion to polluting activity. VED is not a marginal tax but is a fixed cost. An increase in VED would be unfair on those who use the car infrequently and whose pollution contribution is therefore small (Table 3.2).

Table 3.2: Ownership of cars by household income

Household income	No car	One car	Two or more cars
Lowest 25% of households	80%	19%	1%
Second 25%	44%	50%	6%
Third 25%	20%	62%	18%
Highest 25%	7%	46%	47%

Source: National Travel Survey, 1985-86, HMSO

The alternative is to increase taxation on the use of the car, which would initially be by higher taxes on petrol. High petrol prices are a constant incentive to drive fewer miles and to increase fuel economy. Until the sharp increases due to the Gulf crisis the cost of petrol had been falling in real terms since the

1950s (despite the events in 1973 and 1979). Petrol has long been underpriced in relation to rail transport. For someone who owns a car and has paid the annual overheads, a single rail ticket goes only about half the distance as the corresponding quantity of petrol. However the extra car journey causes far more environmental damage than the extra passenger by train.

Our conclusion is that the best way to reduce pollution from car use is a substantial increase in petrol price, combined with regulations for engine efficiency in new vehicles. In the medium term we propose that the cost of VED for private cars be shifted entirely onto petrol duties which are cheap to collect and will thus realise considerable administrative savings.

Duty on petrol and DERV

To encourage greater fuel efficiency and reduced car use, it is therefore necessary for the marginal cost of making an extra car journey to be in line with that of using public transport, and this is our medium term objective. The engine size of a car is not always well related to fuel consumption. Legislation to enforce minimum consumption standards for all new cars and lorries, perhaps related to passenger or freight capacity, could also make a significant impact.

We propose raising the duty by 75p for both petrol and diesel, and maintaining the current differential in favour of unleaded petrol. This is a smaller real increase in duty than we would have chosen in the absence of the Gulf events. Taking account of inflation, the real increase is about 50p.

Substantial, continuing and predictable increases in petrol duty will have the effect of reducing consumption. The Institute for Fiscal Studies (IFS) estimated in 1990* that a 55p rise in petrol duty would cut consumption by 8% initially and by more in later years. We estimate that an increase of 75p in duty would raise just over £5bn in the first year in additional revenue (i.e. after allowing for inflation and assuming the cuts in consumption that the IFS estimated). Less would be raised in following years as motorists adjusted to higher prices and cut consumption.

We would raise petrol and diesel duty by more in subsequent years, until there was substantial equivalence between the costs of travel in private cars and by public transport. A properly balanced transport policy will also require subsidies and other assistance to build up public transport.

Air travel

Air travel poses particular problems because of the airlines' ability to purchase fuel freely outside the UK. Aviation spirit is currently exempt from the duty imposed on petrol and diesel. In gallons of petrol per passenger mile air travel is roughly as wasteful as an average car carrying one person.

We therefore propose to raise the tax on aviation fuel steadily over until it reaches the same level as petrol. If other countries do not match this with similar or equivalent measures, we would require all flights originating in the UK to pay the tax to ensure that international airlines do not seek to avoid the tax by buying elsewhere.

Company cars and commercial vehicles

Company cars contribute more than their fair share to congestion and pollution. They are purchased, or leased, with regard only to their prestige value, their potential for reducing the time spent by expensive executives on the road and their resale value at two years old or less. There is no consideration given to economy or long life. Frequently also a company car is accompanied by the unacceptable perk of unrestricted petrol consumption. We propose to withdraw all tax relief on company cars, replacing it with incentives to use shared transport. This would yield an estimated £0.70bn in annual tax revenue.

Commercial vehicles, in particular articulated or multi-axle lorries, are a major source of environmental concern. Heavy lorries constitute a large and growing environmental problem, not only with unacceptable noise and pollution in built-up areas, but also in tremendous damage to the road structure. Friends of the Earth estimate that a multi-axle lorry does 100,000 times the damage of a private car. We propose increasing the excise duty on heavy goods vehicles over 24 tonnes (approximately 60,000) by 50%. In the medium term a combined tax on weight and distance travelled would be a better way of taxing lorries for the damage and nuisance they cause, and this would be investigated.

Budget proposals

• A carbon fuel tax at a rates of 10%, 8% and 6% on cost price to be applied to all production and import of coal, oil and gas respectively   £1.9bn

• A tax on nitrogen based fertilisers at a rate of 40% on cost price   £0.14bn

• A system of pollution charging to be introduced

• Petrol and diesel duty to be raised by 75p per gallon (after indexation)   £5.1bn

• Vehicle excise duty for commercial vehicles exceeding 24 tonnes to be raised by 50%

• All tax reliefs for company cars to be abolished

£0.7bn

Impact: total additional revenue £7.8bn

Medium term proposals

• Progressive increases in the rate of carbon tax by 2% each year until the year 2000

• Policies monitored by an annual 'carbon audit' to ensure meeting target of 30% cut in greenhouse gas emissions by 2005

• A system of resource taxation on suitable raw materials to be introduced through the EC in stages. To be levied at extraction or import

• Equivalent taxation to be imposed through the EC on imported manufactured goods

• Research and pilot studies into tradeable pollution permits

• Progressive increases in petrol and diesel duty until rough equivalence in marginal cost with public transport is reached

• Tax on aviation fuel to be brought into line with the tax on petrol

4

Indirect Taxation

To put it bluntly - hitting people in their pocket is where it hurts. If you tax something that is bought and sold, people tend to use less of it than they otherwise would, the degree depending on the alternatives available. We believe that indirect taxation offers significant potential to encourage environmentally-responsible behaviour - in the context of proper compensation for the less well-off. Furthermore there is now widespread public support for such measures.

Here we present the Budget proposals for VAT, alcohol and tobacco duties. (Other indirect tax measures are discussed in *Environmental Taxation* and *Transport*). Indirect taxes are those taxes which are not imposed on individuals or firms directly - like income or corporation tax - but are paid indirectly through higher prices. The main indirect taxes on expenditure are Value Added Tax (VAT), car tax and the duties on fuel, tobacco and alcohol.

These are established as important sources of revenue for government and are not primarily conventionally seen as having little purpose other than to raise revenue. In 1988 VAT raised £29bn (18% of total taxation revenue), fuel duties £8bn (5% of total), and tobacco and alcohol duties each about £5bn (3%). Altogether these indirect taxes on expenditure raised around £50bn, about one third of government revenue.

We believe that taxes on income should be lowered relative to taxes on land and on consumption of resources and energy (see *Direct taxation*). We are looking to raise the overall proporation of indirect taxation. We also plan to use these taxes selectively to discourage the production and consumption of goods that are profligate in resources and energy, or are harmful to the environment either in their production or in their disposal.

A common criticism of raising levels of expenditure taxation is that the policy hits those on low incomes hardest. They will need increased incomes just to cover basic needs. This is why taxation and revenue raising cannot be properly considered in isolation from questions of income distribution (see *Introduction*).

Value Added Tax

Nearly two million traders are involved in the collection of VAT for the government, making it probably the most inefficient tax ever used in this country. Radical changes are ruled out by EC membership. However some reforms can be made to make it more environmentally-friendly and to relieve some of the burden it places on small businesses.

At present all businesses with an annual turnover greater than £25,400 have to register for VAT. The keeping of accounts and rendering of VAT returns make heavy demands on the small business, particularly small retailers, and the revenue involved is small compared with the time taken. As an immediate reform we propose that the turnover limit be raised to £40,000. Mechanisms need to be established at the same time for small traders to recoup VAT expenditure. The limit should then be raised further in subsequent years.

VAT is currently charged on the economic value of goods and services alike, without any consideration of the resource or energy intensity. Most services, like repair and maintenance, or hairdressing, are labour-intensive, use very few resources and cause little pollution. In an ideal world we would restructure VAT so that it bears more on the resources and energy added at each stage, and less on the labour content. However we are constrained by EC regulations to a reduced number of options. We can immediately zero-rate repairs for VAT (construction of new dwellings is currently zero-rated). In the medium term we would identify some main classifications of services which would also be zero-rated.

VAT and domestic fuel

At present domestic energy is zero rated for VAT in Britain, unlike the practice in the rest of Europe and the treatment of commercial energy. There is a clear case on conservation grounds for subjecting it to the standard rate. The arguments against are two:

• it taxes the use of benign fuels such as windpower at the same rate as the use of fossil fuels

• it would badly affect the poorer households.

The first argument illustrates the importance of applying resource taxes to specific scarce resources like fossil fuels. However energy as a whole has become too cheap, and Britain has lagged behind most European countries in energy conservation. The second objection is more serious (and is considered in the *Introduction*). But this is no reason why the well-off should continue to enjoy cheap energy when the consequences of energy waste are so great.

We therefore propose that VAT be levied at the standard rate on domestic energy . This has been estimated by the Institute for Fiscal Studies as yielding about £1.7bn annually.[42] We would also consider an energy allowance scheme, so that a first amount or proportion of energy charged for on each bill would be zero-rated. There are clear problems with this, as consideration of multi-fuel and multi-occupant homes will reveal.

Environmental labelling of consumer goods

Environmental labelling of goods is becoming increasingly important, both as a way of informing consumers and as a way of promoting best practice amongst manufacturers and producers. 'Green labelling' of manufactured goods can take into account the following factors: the life of the good in terms of guarantee period offered, whether it is made from recyclable materials, whether minimum packaging is used, whether it is produced using the cleanest technology available, the energy efficiency of the production process. For food and drink, there are the further questions of agricultural chemicals used for production, and additives contained in the final product (this last could cause problems beyond the control of the producers).

A vital step is to have the mandatory energy-efficiency labelling of all electrical appliances. These should be labelled clearly and informatively, indicating compliance with performance standards, together with a comparative indication of the level of efficiency regarded as current good practice and the best state of the art technology.

Germany with its Blue Angel scheme has taken the lead in environmental labelling. It is run by the federal government and covers a wide range of consumer goods. In this country as yet there are only some private schemes operated by supermarkets, one run by the paper industry involving the content of recycled paper, and of course the well known Soil Association symbol for organic produce. There is a proliferation of other symbols, including some which are clearly designed to mislead the consumer.

We propose to establish and monitor a comprehensive Green Labelling Scheme. There are, admittedly, difficulties in establishing standards which are relative both to the product and the state of technology. Nevertheless it is preferable to have some set of national standards than the present anarchy and such a scheme could be operating within a year.

Once the scheme is operating, we propose that goods carrying the new Green Label should be zero-rated for VAT. This will provide further strong incentives for producers to make, and consumers to buy, green-labelled goods. It would be integrated with the proposed EC system for environmental labelling if and when that becomes operational.

Alcohol and tobacco duties

Throughout history mood- and mind-altering substances have been used by people and are likely to continue to be used in one form or another. The extent to which people use drugs in our society depends not only on the price and the availability but also on personal, social, economic and environmental factors. Widespread drug use has a corrosive effect on society and can lead to crime.

In recent years the drug problem has been equated with the use of illegal drugs and attention has been diverted from the dire social and health effects of the legal drugs, principally alcohol and tobacco, which cause the loss of thousands of lives each year and much pain and disability for both users and non-users. We seek to minimise the social, psychological and physical harm to drug users and to society. As with environmental pollution, this form of personal pollution can be significantly discouraged by raising the price.

The rates of duty on alcohol and tobacco have been raised by less than inflation in recent years, possibly because government was concerned about the impact on the Retail Price Index. We believe this concern is misplaced. There is an increasing level of consensus about the harmful effects of smoking. In 1988 the

British Medical Association recommended a substantial increase in tobacco duty, both to catch up with previous years and to curb consumption further. This was not done, and in the 1990 Budget the duties were again not indexed fully.

We propose an immediate increase in tobacco duty of 21%, which would put about 30p on a pack of 20 cigarettes and make the price about the same in real terms as it was in 1948. Assuming an initial fall in consumption of 5%, this would raise about £1.1bn in the first year, or about £0.6bn in extra revenue over and above inflation.

The British Medical Association also proposed raising the duty on tobacco by 6% over the rate of inflation each year for five years, estimating the effect to be a fall in consumption by around 20%, and thus a significant reduction in the cost to the Health Service from all the tobacco-related diseases. This we would also undertake to do over the medium term.

We propose for similar reasons to raise alcohol duties by 15%. With a fall in consumption in the first year of 3%, this would raise about £0.8bn (£0.3bn above inflation). We would also undertake to index the duties with inflation each succeeding year.

Budget proposals

- raise exemption limit for VAT to £40,000 turnover p.a.
- zero-rating of VAT for repairs and Green Label products
- zero-rating for energy efficient appliances, with mandatory labelling of energy use
- domestic energy supply to be positive rated for VAT   £1.7bn
- raise tobacco duty by 21%   £0.6bn
- raise alcohol duty by 15%   £0.3bn

Impact : Extra Revenue £2.5bn (after indexation)

Medium term

- mandatory energy-efficiency labelling of appliances
- identify main VAT categories of services for zero-rating
- raise tobacco duties by 6% over the rate of inflation
- index alcohol duties to inflation
- further raising of VAT limit for small businesses

5

Monetary Policy

A faceful of bricks

Monetary policy describes how the government attempts to influence the amount of money in the economy, how it is created and what it is used for. It has been said that monetary control by interest rates is like pulling a brick along a table with a rubber band. Nothing happens until the brick hits you in the face. The UK economy is experiencing bricks by the faceload.

Since about 1987 the UK economy policy has been going through a crisis period. This is evidenced by the coexistence of high interest rates, endemic inflation,and a large current account deficit.

To those three we must add serious problems on the supply side. There is a desperate need for investment in infrastructure (especially transport and energy), education and training, and conserving technologies of all kinds (see *Introduction*). Such investment will require cuts in consumption of goods and quite possibly new financial instruments. Lasting solutions to all these problems would also help in the supply side deficiencies.

High inflation and current account deficits have both been familiar in the UK since the last war. Inflation has been higher in the UK than in the major EC countries throughout recent history. Figure 5.1 shows the UK current account over the last 25 years together with the North Sea oil contribution to it. It is clear that without North Sea oil the UK slide into deficit would be much greater.

Interest rates have been increased to near-record levels since 1987, and were held at 15% for over a year in 1989-90. In theory high interest rates should squeeze out high inflation by reducing demand, and then correct a balance of payments deficit. They have clearly not succeeded. Instead they have contributed to high levels of consumer debt and have put many small firms in great financial difficulty.

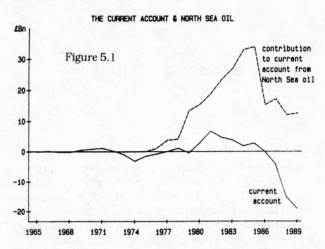

THE CURRENT ACCOUNT & NORTH SEA OIL

Figure 5.1

contribution to current account from North Sea oil

current account

Do high interest rates cure inflation?

The stop-go cycle has been recurrent in recent history, as governments have attempted to steer between the Scylla of recession and the Charybdis of inflation and deficit. Growth in demand in a 'go' period tends to suck in imports, send the current balance into deficit, and increase inflation.

The traditional remedy of high interest rates, imposed in a 'stop' period, aims to curb inflation both by reducing domestic consumer demand and by keeping the currency high by inducing foreigners to send their capital here. However high rates are a dangerous double-edged sword. In the deregulated 1990s there is scarcely such a thing as a national money supply. Money flows internationally from where it is plentiful and cheap to where it is scarce and expensive. So dear money does not become scarce, it becomes plentiful but remains dear.

The policy may have worked for short periods in the past, but at the significant cost of a large number of business closures and steadily increasing unemployment. This was particularly hard in the recession of 1980-81, when a substantial fraction of UK manufacturing industry was lost. Such treatment is not unfairly described as curing the disease by killing the patient.

The diagnosis of the disease is not misplaced. In our Budget we recognise that consumption is indeed too high, and there need to be significant cuts in consumption in order to invest in a sustainable future. The UK has also been consuming too many imported goods. What *is* misplaced is the prescription of high interest rates. Although interest rates have continued at near-record high levels, inflation remains obstinately high and the current account deficit has shown no sign of narrowing.

The conventional analysis ignores the effect that high interest rates have in stoking up inflation. This applies not just to the headline Retail Prices Index (RPI), which includes mortgage rates, but also to underlying or factory gate inflation. Figure 5.2 shows how interest rates have led retail price inflation over the last 30 years. As interest rates have increased, they not only contribute immediately to inflation but also 'stoke up' inflation to come. The pressure on prices then contributes to pressure for higher earnings, and the spiral continues.

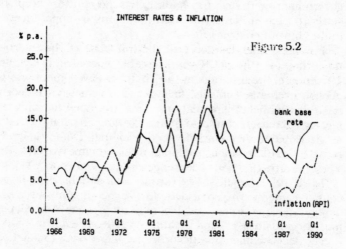

INTEREST RATES & INFLATION

Figure 5.2

A high interest policy has redistributive effects. High rates increase significantly the profits of the lending institutions and, by putting more into the pockets of the well-off, increase their power to buy luxury imports. Dear money thus contributes to the fact that, for the first time in more than a century in the UK, the rich are getting markedly richer while the poor are getting poorer.

If falls in interest rates are now likely, they are for political rather than economic reasons. The ever-present danger is that, unless accompanied by alternative constraints on spending, any reduction would immediately take the lid off consumption, with a further deterioration in the current account, another upward twist in house prices, and yet further inflation. This is the classic dilemma of conventional economic policy.

Roots of the problems

Why should UK economic performance, in conventional terms, be so much worse than her competitors? The monetarist analysis - that the quantity of money in the economy eventually feeds through into prices - is correct as far as it goes. But explanations are needed for why, for instance, demand for money increases when interest rates go up. We need to look at the nature of the banking system, under which money is created predominantly as debt by the main banks, and over which the government or the central bank exerts no control except by setting the base interest rate. Contradictions are apparent even in the conventional view.

Financial liberalisation and the influence of the interna-tiona'rkets over the last 10 years have been decisive. In October 1979 one of the first acts of the Thatcher government was to abolish exchange controls, followed with somewhat indecent haste by financial deregulation. This was done not only for ideological reasons but also from a growing recognition that a single global money market was developing. Domestic credit controls were later abolished for many of the same reasons. The 'corset', restricting banks' lending, was abandoned in 1981.

In the 1980s people showed an almost insatiable demand for consumer credit. This coincided with the government's sweeping deregulation in the personal debt markets. As banks developed mortgage businesses, and building societies became more like banks, debt became a product to be sold aggressively to consumers - 'taking the waiting out of wanting'.

Although monetarism was supposedly the government's guiding star, by the mid-1980s monetary targets had been abandoned. The money supply grew strongly, but inflation stayed low. This led to a false sense of security in the Treasury. Asset prices, and house prices in particular, soared as people realised that mortgage interest payments were small relative to the capital gain they could make without penalty in the housing market.

Banks found it easy to attract funds and make loans in the liberalising global money markets. Simultaneously, demand for borrowing was little deterred by high interest rates as surging house and asset prices imparted a misleading sense of personal wealth. People started to withdraw the equity in their house by taking a second mortgage and buying a second car. For instance, in the ten years from 1978, annual net loans for house purchase increased from £5bn to £41bn. However an estimated £25bn of that £41 bn was actually equity withdrawal, not for house purchase.[34]

Under these circumstances it was still profitable to lend, even though credit was expensive, and so banks bid more aggressively for customers' deposits. High interest rates, far from discouraging new lending, in many cases therefore stimulated it.

The short-termism of the financial system has been much discussed, and comparisons have been made with (say) Germany or Japan. In Germany the banks take a much more active role in the companies they give financial support to, often taking seats on the board. They can be said to nurse their companies from the cradle to, if not the grave, then at least to mid-life. In the UK, by contrast, the frequent complaint from small business, in particular, is that banks have no care for the general health and welfare of the company they lend to, only for their security in the event of bankruptcy.

A recent report from the Centre for Economic Policy Research recommends that banks should be encouraged to take equity positions and to get more involved in company finance.[33] Both the Institute for Public Policy Research (IPPR) - on the political left - and the Institute for Economic Affairs (IEA) - on the political right - have both recently published reports on the shortcomings of the financial system! The IEA document notes that the ownership of Britain's leading companies is in the hands of 150 fund managers, who 'treat shares like any other commodity'.[52] The IPPR reports the views of leading company directors that withdrawal from the stock market would be the best solution for companies who are trying to pursue long term objectives.[25]

We conclude that the banks use their monopoly to create money by lending on credit in ways which are often inimical to the interests of both the community and the environment. There certainly has been no thought as to whether the purpose of the loan was for unsustainable consumption or for environmentally appropriate investment. The system must be replaced by one in which institutions are accountable to the community, and responsive to its needs.

A green monetary policy

One possible response is to seek to nationalise the banks. However this could have the effect of replacing an irresponsible but relatively efficient system with one more bureaucratic, less efficient and only marginally more responsible. A green monetary policy provides a route to an alternative financial architecture in which institutions serve the wider interest, rather than the narrow. It would seek to offer these features:

• a hierarchy of levels of monetary policy
• a commitment at the highest level to monetary stability
• differentiation of monetary targets by level
• local monetary autonomy within limits set by the higher levels
• financial institutions accountable locally
• local credit responsive to local needs
• incentives to save and invest in the local economy and in sustainable technologies
• social and environmental auditing of all loans and investment.

In a green framework, tight overall monetary control would coexist with monetary growth at the local level. A tight, but appropriately targetted, monetary policy would make it harder to get a loan to buy a new car, for instance, but easier for a small socially- and environmentally- friendly firm to obtain start-up capital. There need to be controls and audits of potential loans to insure against irresponsible money-lending. Banks should be accountable to the community for how they operate.

Monetary policy would therefore be differential in its impact, aiming to stimulate local demand for locally produced goods and services and investment demand in suitable areas, while at the same time discouraging growth in demand for consumer and imported goods. It would rely more on supply side pressures on the commercial banks and building societies to control credit, than on the blunderbuss weapon of base lending rates.

Existing institutions
and commercial interest rates

Commercial interest rates will need to remain high, until supply-side measures of credit control take effect. They would coexist with concessional rates available from new non profit-making financial institutions.

Overall tightness in policy would be reinforced by the reintroduction of minimum reserve requirements for banks, under which the clearing banks have to place a certain proportion of their assets on deposit with the Bank of England. (Minimum reserve requirements are operated in every country on mainland Europe except Luxembourg).

At the same time it will be necessary to restrict borrowing for consumption and house purchase. Therefore personal credit controls will also be necessary. These will take the form of restrictions on legally-recoverable personal debt to a certain fraction of annual income - we propose 30%. Individuals would be free to borrow more than that amount, but the onus would be on the lender to check that the loan did not bring the total above the legally-recoverable amount. These measures would dampen the enthusiasm with which lenders currently chase borrowers.

Tighter capital adequacy limits must also be used as a way of restricting bank and building society lending. More directive guidance to banks and building societies can be given as to the amount and purpose of lending and the security needed. The risk attached to mortgage lending could be increased by various measures and mortgage tax relief must be limited and reduced[47] (see *Direct taxation*).

New institutions

A green approach would involve a programme of practical decentralisation of banking and monetary policy, linked with a programme of political devolution (see *Local government*). It will need new financial institutions that offer a greater degree of social and political accountability. Of paramount importance to this policy will be a network of local community banks largely replacing in the long term the operations of the commercial clearing banks (see *The local economy*).

Statutory non-profit regional investment banks could provide support for the community banks in their areas, for instance by providing software, expertise and help in carrying out environmental impact studies. Community and regional banks would be governed by boards of trustees accountable to various sections of the (appropriate) community. In many areas they could be set up as banking arms of already existing local economic development bodies. Under a banking system more committed to the local economy, debt finance might be replaced by a greater measure of equity finance. Community banks, with a full understanding and support for local projects, could offer concessionary rates of interest to appropriate local firms.

These proposed new publicly-owned financial institutions would require start-up capital. The government would supply some, but it would be right to expect a contribution from the private sector. There is therefore a good case for mandatory deposits from existing financial institutions, possibly as a percentage of turnover. This would help to redirect investment money in a simple and dramatic way, and would reduce inflationary pressures, while at the same time not destroying the confidence of existing institutions.

In the financing of government capital spending we propose that in the long term all levels of government should be able to obtain a proportion of capital needs direct from their own banking systems. There should also be a programme to write off that proportion of public debt which is owed to the banking system.

The UK and economic and monetary union (EMU)

The near-fixed exchange rates in the exchange rate mechanism (ERM) offer the prospect of short-term stability but involve the loss of considerable autonomy in monetary policy. Monetary union would complete the process by effectively replacing national central banks with a European central bank, taking away all remaining national freedom to set interest rates and influence money supply.

The compromise plan of the 'hard ECU', outlined by the British Chancellor of the Exchequer in 1990, has considerable potential merits. It offers the prospect of a Europe-wide hard currency which operates side by side with national currencies. Such a scheme could work alongside the differentiated multi-level global monetary system which will be necessary for a green decentralised economy to function. Firms and people who need to trade outside the local economy would use the appropriate hard currency. Those who worked and traded within the locality or region may use a more local, and softer, currency.

There are clearly potential problems with parallel currencies, chiefly from the danger that the local currencies become progressively devalued. However these should not deter us from developing and promoting such schemes in the medium term, both in localities and possibly Europe-wide.

External constraints

The most important constraint on a green monetary policy is of course the external constraint of a worldwide market. This means that UK interest rates (in real terms, i.e. after allowing for inflation) cannot stray too far from those in our main trading partners without triggering large jumps in the exchange rate. With the UK a member of the ERM, the freedom of manoeuvre is limited even further.

The main external constraint is the huge current balance of payments deficit amounting to nearly £20bn in 1990. This means that the UK lives off the rest of the world to that amount in goods and services every year. The pound is only supported by inflows of 'hot' short-term money looking for returns from our high interest rates. This cannot go on indefinitely; at some point all the land and capital that foreigners wish to buy will have been sold.

Economic theory suggests a devaluation of the pound, making imports more expensive and UK exports more competitive, together with a squeeze on spending. Devaluation by itself does not inhibit imports, it only boosts inflation. This traditional prescription may well not be enough to reduce the UK appetite for foreign goods.

Our preference is therefore for devaluation, accompanied by a continued tight monetary policy. A reasonable rate for sterling in the medium term might be in the range DM2.60 to DM2.80, higher than a 'deep discount' which would immediately boost inflation, but low enough to begin the painful process of helping to correct the balance of payment deficit .

The objection is frequently made that credit controls would not work because people could simply borrow abroad, now that there are no longer exchange controls. However, in European countries where credit controls do operate, the experience is that they are effective to a significant degree even without exchange controls. In addition we would examine the possibility of reintroduction of controls on the movement of capital, or more general exchange controls. The latter could operate for instance by a percentage tax on currency exchange. This would be relatively simple to operate, hard (for banks) to evade, and would act as a marginal discouragement to seeking credit abroad. However, such a measure would require a withdrawal of the undertaking the UK made in respect of the Single Market.

We have to accept the UK membership of the ERM as a reality in the medium-term. Nevertheless the Delors plans for economic and monetary union should be firmly opposed, as a grave threat to regional and local autonomy in Europe.

"The poor are getting poorer, but with the rich getting richer it all averages out in the long run."

Budget proposals

- Continued high commercial interest rates over the short term
- Minimum reserve requirements for banks and building societies
- Tighter capital adequacy and direction on lending by banks and building societies
- Personal credit legislation to limit legally-recoverable debt to 30% of gross annual income
- Legislation for community banks, municipal banks and regional investment banks, to provide investment and low interest loans to business
- Opposition to economic and monetary union in the EC
- Qualified acceptance of entry into the ERM but seek realignment at a rate between DM2.60 to DM2.80

Medium-term proposals

- Nationwide network of community banks, municipal banks and regional investment banks
- Mandatory percentage contributions to community and regional banks from financial institutions
- Loans and investment from community and regional banks to be subject to social and environmental audits
- Investigation of capital and more general exchange controls
- The phased writing-off of all public debt owed to the banking system

6

Energy

The Green Budget seeks to address the problems of energy pollution by minimising consumption, maximising efficiency, and using renewable, non-polluting sources to satisfy the remaining demand. We have to move beyond thinking of individual businesses in competition supplying energy to make profits. What people need is warmth, heat and power in the right proportions and in the right places. The future lies in reducing energy demand, and in greening the supply of energy by harnessing the abundant renewable sources available.

The new thinking considers the whole picture, in terms of the best way for society to meet the energy needs of the people. The short term thinking that currently dominates government policy has ruled out large scale energy efficiency measures. The energy utilities have been sold with the emphasis solely on the requirement to make profits. Energy efficiency could have an adverse effect on those profits in the short term.

The requirement to cut drastically the burning of fossil fuels as part of a strategy to stabilise the global climate brings many other benefits. The more efficient use of energy will enhance global security by reducing the dependence of oil-importing countries on Middle Eastern oil. Similarly a national programme of home insulation will result in fewer deaths from hypothermia, as the old and the poor use less fuel to keep warm and their fuel bills are reduced.

Nuclear power - too costly to contemplate

Energy generated by nuclear power can be ruled out of any serious future energy supply scenarios. Putting aside the major worries about safety and the still unresolved waste problems, nuclear power is inappropriate on strategic, cost-efficiency and energy efficiency grounds alone.

The proposed replacement of coal-fired stations to reduce CO_2 production even in the International Panel on Climate Change (IPCC) scenario for future energy needs would be impossible in both physical and energy terms. It would mean building an average 1 gigawatt plant every two and a half days for the next 35 years!

Full practical use of the best oil and gas saving technologies (either already on or coming onto the market in the next 5 years) could save upto threequarters of oil used now. It is already clear that every £1 invested in cutting out waste and using energy efficiently reduces the amount of CO_2 produced by 7 times more than if it were invested in nuclear power.

Restraining energy demand

The short-term measures that must be taken to reduce energy consumption are discussed under carbon taxation in *Environmental taxation*. Changes to indirect taxation are equally important. Proposals for levying VAT on energy and exemption for energy efficiency improvements are detailed in *Indirect taxation*. Investment in energy conservation is a further major step. Energy Conservation Grants to householders will be reinstated and widened and made applicable to industry and all commercial firms. Approximately threequarters of this investment should be in the form of grants. Eligible measures to improve space heating efficiency would include:-

• upgrading wall, ceiling and floor insulation, to meet new standards of thermal performance for buildings .

• ventilation control such as draughtproofing

• improved heating controls, such as thermostats, time clocks, optimisers and compensators, and the zoning of heating systems in the service and industrial sectors.

Commercial and institutional properties will require surveys to prove efficiency before Conservation Grants are awarded. The Extended Energy Survey Scheme grants will be reinstated to enable a two part consultant's report to be prepared; the first part to identify the low or no-cost 'good housekeeping' measures which must first be implemented and the second to identify the proposed capital schemes necessary to reduce the level of energy consumption still further.

We also propose that a start be made on a crash programme

of systematic household insulation, aiming initially at poorer households, as recently argued by Right To Fuel, Neighbourhood Energy Action, Heatwise Glasgow and Friends of the Earth.[54] Their plan proposed upgrading to 1990 insulation standards the homes of 500,000 low income households each year until 2005. The annual cost was estimated to be £1.25bn.

An instant attack on both fuel poverty and waste can be made with the issue of free long-life and energy-efficient light bulbs to every pensioner and claimant for income support (as has been done in the U.S. by energy utilities).

The Department of Energy's own reports advocate spending £1.5bn annually on conservation measures; the above proposals involve spending £1.5bn on all conservation-related measures per year for the next five years.

A final area for action is to set new standards for the thermal performance of buildings. Although only introduced in 1990, the relevant section of the Buildings Regulations was drafted in 1986 and is now quite inadequate. These standards must be radically upgraded, and expressed as thermal performance values (the amount of permissible heat loss per cubic metre p.a.). The National Home Energy Rating Scheme, which uses this approach, should be extended to other sectors. Its certified ratings should be accepted as proof that a building achieves the new standards.

The proposal that a National Energy Index be published annually is discussed in *Objectives*.

Greening energy supply: short term measures

Even if privatisation of the remaining electricity supply industry goes ahead, the national grid company must be brought back into public control. In a publicly owned distribution system the distributor can be empowered to refuse to accept supply from inappropriate, high cost sources, while working alongside the agency which coordinates the conservation programme.

Another important benefit can be realised by changing the rules to impose 'least cost integrated planning' on electricity supply companies and the proposed new District Energy Authorities (see below). 'Least cost planning' requires the utilities to prioritise the provision of energy services with the least cost investment, rather than to maximise profits or make a given return on capital. This has been established with much success in parts of the US with the cheaper energy prices attracting new businesses so that high street shops prosper significantly in comparison with towns nearby.[18]

The cost of producing energy from renewable sources is tumbling. Already wind can generate electricity at around 3-4p per KwH against the nuclear claim of 2.5-3p per KwH, and way below the acknowledged real cost of nuclear in both the US and UK of around 7-8p. Similarly costs of generating electricity directly from solar cells (photovoltaics) have dropped dramatically from around £30 per KwH in 1970 to between 10p and 20p today. The new technology of solar cells shows the potential for very low costs indeed.[55] Already energy directly from the sun delivers light, heat and power through solar cells to remote homes and communities throughout the world.

The present UK investment programme spends £159.3m on nuclear power and £17.4m on renewable sources of energy. To make up for lost time there must be an immediate investment of £300m, continued annually, to establish a vigorous development programme for renewable energy projects. From years 2 to 5, expenditure would be offset by £100m by a reduction of the research budget for nuclear power.

Tax incentives for companies investing in new equipment would be brought in. These would be for investments such as:

• installing small scale combined heat and power (CHP) stations for their own use
• CHP schemes using their wastes as an energy source
• replacement of electric resistance heating by heat pumps
• installation of solar heating
• replacement of conventional oil and gas central heating boilers with high-efficiency condensing boilers.

Turning thermo generated electricity back into space heating make a nonsense of the laws of nature. Free credit for installation of off-peak electric heating must therefore be stopped and new on-peak electric heating must be banned.

One added advantage of the proposed carbon tax (see *Environmental taxation*) is that cost of electricity from fossil-fuelled sources to the electricity supply companies would increase. The level of carbon tax would be such as to ensure that the 'buy-back tariff' (the price paid for electricity to people who run their own generators and sell the surplus to the grid) produces an adequate commercial rate of return on investment in renewable sources of energy. Such an arrangement would not infringe EC controls on competition.

Energy tariffs for consumers have been producing absurd results. Some commercial users of gas flared off gas (the 'flame of shame') to qualify for lower bulk tariffs, and some Local Education Authorities required schools to put on their heating during the holidays for the same reason. British Gas has reformed its tariff structures to cancel out the effect of lower unit cost thresholds, but tariffs must be further reformed so that bulk users pay more, not less, for their fuel. This would help small businesses and concentrate the minds of large users on investment in energy saving measures.

Greening energy supply: medium term measures

As part of the constitutional reform of local government, we propose that new District Energy Authorities be established under local authority control. For many years the UN has said that energy planning is one of the most important roles of local authorities. A land-use plan may be more or less energy efficient depending on the settlement pattern and the way it generates the need for transport movement.

Local authorities are directly responsible for waste collection and disposal, and building regulations, as well as the use of their own buildings. They are well placed to integrate strategic planning with their other functions and influence the private sector. In particular they would be responsible for drawing up district heating schemes in areas of sufficient population density. In the medium term District Energy Authorities would be required to prepare strategic energy plans and to institute energy audits to show how much non-renewable energy the UK uses, and encourage decreasing use.

It would be practicable for 600 MW of electricity generating capacity to be fuelled from waste sources by the year 2000, and about 400 MW from organic wastes if collected separately from refuse. About two thirds of this could be from waste incineration plants in the conurbations and the rest from methane extraction at large landfill sites.

Penalties will be imposed on uncontrolled emissions of landfill gas, and refuse collection and disposal will be reorganised to minimise the wasteful dumping of potentially useful refuse. Smaller scale schemes capable of collecting and using landfill gas from the hundreds of smaller sites are needed.

There is still some uncertainty about the best technology for managing waste, and it must be remembered that recycling, together with the composting or digestion of biodegradable material, may be preferable to incineration. An audit of environmental and economic factors is needed.

Renewable energy sources could eventually meet all of our electricity needs. The reform of electricity buy-back tariffs and the local authority rating of small scale energy producers is essential. Having created the right institutional framework, the rate of introduction of renewable energy production is influenced only by local siting factors, manufacturing capabilities and political will.

The UK has one of the best wind energy resources in the world. It is estimated that on-shore wind power could produce 20% of Britain's electricity needs. Off-shore wind power, with fewer environmental constraints, could contribute a further 60%. The intermittent nature of wind means that there are limits to the proportion that it alone can provide. Large scale off-shore wave power sources are particularly suitable for integration with off-shore wind power because of time-lags between the peaks of wind and wave energy. An EC commissioned study estimated in 1986 that wave resource of the Atlantic coast of Europe is equivalent to 85% of total EC electricity demand!

The key task of the central energy authority is to integrate renewable sources of electricity into a balanced energy strategy, with District Energy Authorities playing a crucial role at the local level. There is a large employment potential with all energy efficiency and conservation measures and more so in the design and construction of renewable energy mechanisms. Wind and wave power devices, and waste incineration programmes, are particularly suitable for the proposed conversion of the economic, scientific and technological resources presently used to support the arms race, such as shipbuilding, aerospace, and power engineering.

Budget proposals

- 10 year energy conservation programme to be started
  £1.7bn
- Above programme to include free insulation and low-energy light bulbs to low-income households
- Extra resources for renewable energy development
  £0.3bn
- Rundown of nuclear power investment programme
- Building regulations to be revised
- Energy tariffs to be reformed

Impact : £2.0bn

Medium term proposals

- Continual monitoring of emissions from all pollutants and greenhouse gases. Revision of taxation rates and investment spending to meet targets
- A continuing audit of environmental and economic factors involved in the generation of energy from waste

7

Transport spending

Conventional thinking has assumed that more transport equals progress. A sustainable economic strategy must reject this. It is not enough to try to minimise the harmful effects of transport - the necessity for the current levels of both travel and trade has to be examined. No Green Budget can bring about the necessary changes overnight but we can give clear signals to everybody involved in transport planning and technology that rapid change is required.

There are three major problems associated with the current transport system:
- pollution from exhaust emissions
- land and resources taken up for road transport
- impact on quality of life.

Road accidents cause 5000 deaths and 40,000 injuries annually, and are a major cause of death for children. Each year an estimated 4,000 acres of rural land are lost to road building and each mile of motorway takes 25 acres. Often land in its wildest state is taken for road building, because it shows up as the cheapest option on the Department of Transport's cost-benefit studies.

Transport planning

In the 1989 White Paper *Roads to Prosperity*, the Department of Transport projected a doubling in the number of miles travelled by car in the next 35 years. This would require an estimated area the size of Berkshire just to park the extra cars. This highlights the cul de sac into which British transport policy has driven, especially when considered in the global context. That the government can consider accommodating these increases shows culpable complacency.

In the medium term the strategy must be to:
- reduce the need for transport in the economy
- introduce or rejuvenate low energy, mass transport systems
- ensure that resulting private and public transport meets environmental and social targets.

A rational transport strategy must be aimed primarily at tackling those conditions in which the car and the lorry become necessary and flourish, rather than at the vehicles themselves. The overall aim must be to make the private car and road haulage increasingly unnecessary, both by reducing the needs for transport and by making the alternatives available, affordable and pleasant. The reduction of car use and fuel consumption must be the target, within the context of a balanced transport policy.

To carry out this strategy will require a twofold revolution in how transport is planned and funded. Firstly, national strategy would balance the transport needs of the whole community against environmental and social factors, and ensure funding was allocated to the various modes accordingly. A national transport plan can show how, for example, the transport sector will play its part in achieving target reductions in national CO_2 emissions. No longer would there be the absurd situation where the Department of the Environment proclaims a target for CO_2 reductions, while the Department of Transport plans for increases in road traffic which make nonsense of that target.

Secondly, integrated transport planning would be introduced at local and regional levels of government. As local economies become more self-reliant, with far greater local marketing for local needs and integrated local planning for business and residential services, so the transport requirement will be significantly reduced. Local and regional government can work to speed the coordination of these objectives.

Rural car-owners, for whom there are few available alternatives to car use, are of special concern. The best way of helping these people is to regenerate the rural economy so that people will have less far to travel for work or necessity. Ways of doing this would be investigated, such as channelling some petrol revenues into organisations like the Council for Industries in Rural Areas.

Road spending and the Department of Transport

The 1989 Government White Paper *Roads to Prosperity* announced a ten year road-building programme worth over £17bn (1990 prices). The money is to be used for new roads or the widening of existing ones, and is extra to the normal budget for road maintenance. It applies to trunk roads only (motorways and A-roads).

The most immediate priority is to scrap the whole programme. There may be a few exceptions, such as local by-passes, but each case must be stringently proved. The money saved would be redirected into areas such as subsidised rail and water freight, urban mass transit and rural bus and rail. The Transport Supplementary Grant, which funds local authority expenditure, would be restructured to remove the bias towards roads spending.

Other controls on road vehicles

New British cars are the dirtiest in Europe. Not only should car use be reduced, but it should be made as clean as possible. In the long term, investment in the development of clean fuel burning engines for methane or hydrogen offers good possibilities. In the short term much must be done to clean up petrol and diesel engines.

Catalytic converters, as favoured by the EC, reduce the nastier pollutants, but at the expense of reducing engine efficiency and increasing emissions of carbon dioxide (the main contributor to the greenhouse effect). A badly tuned car fitted with a catalytic converter can produce even more pollution than before. Converters are therefore no answer - the UK government's preference for lean burn engines was well-founded.

We propose reducing the maximum speed limit on roads to 55 mph to reduce fuel consumption; this will also reduce the wear and tear on road surfaces and bridge structures that cause high maintenance costs.

Road pricing individual areas of road by electronic means may prove too complicated or expensive to justify. Simpler alternatives, such as traffic-calming measures - e.g. widened pavements and sleeping policemen - would make the streets people-friendly at a fraction of the cost. This does not rule out entry-pricing on a larger scale, under which motorists (except residents) would be charged on entry to a particular city or town. We would investigate this, particularly for London.

There are many ways to share vehicles, reducing the total number required and the number on the road at one time. Car sharing schemes, together with entry pricing and improved park and ride systems, would reduce city congestion and parking problems. Vehicle hire also decreases car use and would be encouraged.

Public transport

Public transport (in the sense that it is available to all, not necessarily publicly owned) is vital to transport policy. Spending on new roads would be switched to developing all aspects of the shared transport sector.

In the medium term a proper investment programme for public transport must be introduced, under which investments in bus, rail and tram schemes can be assessed for the benefits they provide for users, the surrounding community and the environment. British rail investment would be included, and the need for rail investment to show a given return on capital would be removed. Public transport would (again) be regarded as public services, into which investment is seen as providing gains other than profits.

Areas for additional spending would include

• urban transport schemes (tram and rail, overhead monorail, 'maglev')

• grants to bus manufacturers and operators to improve the efficiency, comfort accessibility of buses

• rural bus and rail services

• park and ride schemes

• rail freight.

The cities of Sheffield, Bristol and Manchester are already going ahead with schemes for the reintroduction of trams, and about fifty towns and cities have plans in some form. Trams, though expensive, are far cheaper than underground rail and have fewer disadvantages than buses on city streets.

The Channel tunnel

The rationale of the Channel Tunnel has been seen in terms of promoting more transport, of encouraging more people and goods to cross the Channel. The commercial pressure is not only for a link, but a high speed link. High-speed travel by train leads to a desire to travel fast for the whole journey, so as not to lose the time saved (or bought), and thus to pressure on the local environment at all stages of the journey.

The tunnel rail link has been designed to carry cars and lorries. Although we recognise the link as inevitable in some form, we propose that it be converted to carry passengers (without vehicles) and rail freight only. This measure, accompanied by other incentives to move freight by rail, would be likely to bring a substantial shift from road haulage.

Budget proposals

- Redirection of the money saved by abandoning the £17bn programme for new trunk roads into improvements for rail freight and public transport
- Restructuring the Transport Supplementary Grant for local authority transport expenditure
- Revenues from increased petrol duty to be recycled into public transport improvements and compensation for low income groups
- Transport research funds to be redirected into clean fuel engines
- Grants available for organisations like the Council for Industries in Rural Areas
- Maximum speed limit on roads reduced to 55 mph
- Grants for the investigation of entry-pricing in major cities

Impact: Net revenue: Nil

Medium term measures

- Restructuring the Department of Transport and transport planning in the interests of a balanced transport policy and environmental constraints
- Strategic planning at local and regional level for reduced transport needs by means of a greater localisation of economies
- Minimum standards of fuel consumption for all new vehicles
- A combined weight and distance tax for heavy lorries to be investigated

8

Defence

Military spending

The UK is one of the six biggest spenders on arms in the world. The Ministry of Defence (MoD) controls a budget of over £21bn, 11% of UK land area, over 300,000 armed services personnel and over 50% of government research expenditure. Many jobs depend on MoD contracts and overseas orders for arms. Many people believe that the UK commitment to a civil nuclear power programme (one of the most expensive mistakes ever made) was the result of MoD pressure.

All the talent and resources sequestered by the MoD are denied to the productive economy and this, coupled with the loss of so many able people, civilian and conscript alike, during World War II has had a strong negative impact on our economic development. Comparisons are frequently made with Japan which spends only 5% of its research and development budget on the military sector.

Globally the arms industry is immense. In 1985 global military expenditures were approximately US $850bn. While world GDP increased at an annual rate of 2.4%, military expenditure increased by 3.2% per annum between 1980 and 1985. It is clear that the waste of money, human skills and natural resources is getting worse, not better.

All this was justified by the Cold War, now officially over, so attention has turned to the potential savings to be had through cuts in the defence budget. We must avoid replacing the East/West conflict threat with a substitute manufactured out of the crisis in the Middle East. From a Green perspective, defence cuts are an over-riding priority.

Policy for defence cuts

The present rate of environmental destruction threatens survival and security everywhere on Earth. Conflicts over control of food supplies or mineral deposits are as old as history but no less likely in the future. They must be met effectively by cooperative non-violent responses. The route to common security for all lies in the progressive reduction world wide and eventual abolition by treaty of all offensive weaponry. It will be impossible to move towards a sustainable economy whilst such a staggeringly huge proportion of the world's resources are being eaten up by the military. It really must be time for a change.

Immediate and unconditional nuclear disarmament has to be accepted as a priority on both moral and legal grounds. Similarly the arms trade will not be an acceptable part of a Green economy. Increasing world poverty and militarisation go hand in hand. As one of the world's largest arms exporters, the UK role in the international arms trade is morally abhorrent and has a devastating impact on the Third World where currently three-quarters of UK arms exports go.

The many overseas commitments must be severely reduced. The British Army of the Rhine can be immediately withdrawn, with the phased withdrawal and restructuring from offensive to more defensive postures of other 'out of area' forces. Military aid to other countries can be pruned. The number of military training exercises, particularly overseas, can be considerably reduced. Low flying exercises, especially over land, can be cut back, and the number of RAF squadrons reduced. New equipment and replacement orders can be cut back. The Trident programme can be cancelled immediately, as can the Tactical Air to Surface Missile (TASM) programme. Polaris submarines and Royal Navy Aircraft carriers can be decommissioned.

Defensive defence

The removal of the nuclear threat is not an excuse to build up conventional forces. Our proposal is based on the ability to retain a viable conventional defence capability, by adopting a purely non-offensive stance in weapons deployment. Because it is cheaper to destroy offensive weapons systems than it is to make and deploy them, a non-offensive defence force will be far less of a drain on Britain's limited resources. Moreover defensive defence does not have to be based on highly centralised technologies.

Emphasis will be placed on simply-operated and expendable missiles, cheap to produce in large quantities. Also Britain can maximise the advantage of being an island by relying on strong coastal and anti-aircraft defence, interceptor fighter aircraft and a navy made up of short range coastal defence craft and submarines. Above all, defence must be relatively safe for the people and the territory defended.

In the longer term, a programme of non-violent 'social defence' can be started. This includes training citizens in the use of psychological, moral and political pressure to achieve the kind of 'people power' demonstrated in Eastern Europe. This must be rooted in the kind of self-reliant democratic communities that we seek to promote. Alongside this must be an investment in the capacity of all future generations to achieve and maintain security through the use of peaceful and non-violent means of conflict resolution.

Seeking the 'peace dividend'

It has become common to assume that cutting the defence budget will make untold riches available to rescue the crumbling public services of health, education and welfare. At least one study has been produced demonstrating the potential for 50% cuts whilst still maintaining traditional force structures and nuclear capability and no shift in defence priorities.[7] The potential for high levels of saving, the 'peace dividend', is therefore widely acknowledged.

The sort of programme we propose for defence spending includes nuclear disarmament. Figures produced by the Campaign for Nuclear Disarmament suggest that cuts of up to 60% could be achieved by such a programme. However, the removal of nuclear weapons requires a complete shift from a strategy based on the much questioned concept of nuclear deterrence towards one based on 'defensive defence'. Such restructuring does not come cheap, and must be implemented from the beginning of the nuclear disarmament programme. The Green budget proposals are therefore based on accepting the need for a full programme of concurrent restructuring. This implies that defence spending cuts can only be expected to release a total of 50% for other purposes at the end of a ten year programme providing cumulative savings of £65bn.

Arms conversion

Green principles promote a shift away from destructive or inefficient industries towards a cleaner economy. There is no question but that the conversion of arms manufacture to more socially and environmentally useful work will form a centrepiece in this process, and will provide a great challenge.

Most studies show that disarmament need not lead to greater unemployment, or disruption of the economy. So long as the overall level of economic activity is maintained to allow for the reduction in defence spending, and specific assistance is given to regions particularly heavily affected, the economy will become far healthier. This is for two reasons:

- defence spending may have added significantly to GNP, but the capital is invested in destruction. The equivalent contribution to the nation's wealth directed towards production and construction for environmentally and socially positive work is a real gain

- defence jobs cost far more per job than jobs in other industries, because defence jobs depend on large spending on extremely expensive capital equipment with a very short life. More useful, satisfying work can be provided for the same number of people for considerably less money, making capital investment go much further.

Budget proposals
- Immediate cut in military spending of 5%

  revenue £1.0bn
- Establishment of defence conversion agency, with funding in first year of £0.5bn cost £0.5bn

Net Revenue impact: £0.5bn

Medium Term

- cuts in military spending to increase to 50% over 1990 levels by the year 2000
- Defence Conversion Agency to double scale of its operation over three years

---

9

Agriculture and the countryside

Would you choose a career that landed you dramatically in debt while the results of your efforts commanded ever higher prices in the shops and society viewed you as making yourself rich at the expense of the poor consumers?

A quarter of all farms are running at a loss. A third of farmers derive half their family income from other employment, or from their pensions or savings. Over two-thirds of farms are in debt; a high proportion of loans is 'short money' which can be recalled at short notice. Average borrowings are increasing and were over £58,000 in 1990. Farmers are near the top of the list of those most at risk of suicide, and the number of bankruptcies is rising. This is a catalogue of disaster for the farmer, for the economy, and for our countryside.

British agriculture is characterised by intensive use of land, especially in the south and east of England, by over-production of food, and shrinking farm incomes. These problems are common throughout the Western industrialised countries. In the European Community (EC) the price support operations of the Common Agricultural Policy (CAP) have made them significantly worse.

The industrialisation of agriculture has also led to a general increase in the size of holdings and to widespread control of farming by big business and financial institutions such as pension funds, with little or no interest in the land other than profit. Water pollution from nitrogenous fertilisers is widespread, and the effects of pesticide residues and additives to animal feed on human health are now causing considerable concern.

Small farmers have not benefited from the huge sums spent to support agriculture. This applies not only in the more marginal areas like hill farms, but also to most lowland farms except dairy units. Average net annual income on very small farms in 1988 was only £300 in England and was actually negative in Wales. A third of farms working in 1970 have disappeared in the last twenty years. According to the EC, about 50,000 full-time farmers in the UK, a third of the current total, are expected (i.e. will be forced) to leave agriculture in the next few years. Figure 9.1 shows the loss of workforce in agriculture in the past 140 years.

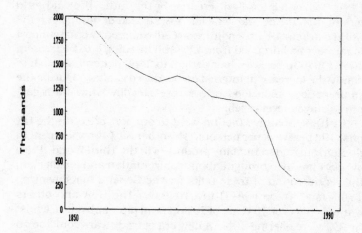

Figure 9.1. People working on farms, full and part-time

The pressure on the countryside has led to some dramatic changes. For example, over the last 40 years half the river meadows and coastal marshes have been converted to arable farming and 110,000 miles of hedgerows have been lost, encouraged until recently by a system of grants and subsidies from the Ministry of Agriculture. Nearly one half of British arable land is now vulnerable to soil erosion, according to Lawrence Woodward of the Soil Association.

A new direction is therefore needed. Farming practice has to move away from increasing soil erosion and pollution. At the same time farmers, particularly the more vulnerable small farmers, need substantial protection during the process of change. The aim must be a thriving rural economy based on an integration of food production, ecology, and recreation, where farming can flourish and the countryside be enhanced. The measures required will be wide-ranging, and will require the reorganisation of several government departments.

Price support versus the environment

The CAP operates a system of guaranteed farm-gate prices for selected products intended to cushion farm incomes and food prices in a world of unpredictable seasons and markets.

As a policy it is totally discredited by the butter, beef and grain mountains, the oil and wine lakes destroyed or dumped on the world markets. UK expenditure on CAP commodity price support to farmers has dropped from £1.84bn in 1985/6 to £1.00bn in 1989/90 (63p per week per person to 34p), not even enough to defray the increase in interest on borrowed capital.[2] During the same period, shop food prices rose steadily while farm-gate prices stayed level or fell.

In 1989/90 only £0.56bn went to support prices in the UK (just 19p per week per person). The other £0.44bn was spent in dumping to undercut many producers in the Third World. Price support has also brought about confrontation and deadlock in the recent round of trade talks for the General Agreement on Tariffs and Trade (GATT) in Uruguay. The USA and others wanted cuts over 10 years of 75% in farm price subsidies, whilst the EC were offering 30%. A new era of trade wars could be on the horizon, even though the USA, Canada, Australia and Europe are busy offering the USSR hard currency loans at competitive prices to buy cereals.[20]

A recent report proposed that the whole system of EC price support be converted to one in which farmers are paid 'environment management payments'.[29] These would be based on the real, measurable environmental benefits that farmland provides, and would not merely be compensation for not polluting or not destroying wildlife habitats. The payments would be decoupled from food production.

We support this proposal as a medium term goal for the reform of the CAP. In the short term we propose that a start be made by devoting all cuts in subsidies agreed in the GATT negotiations to such a scheme. We also propose that the set-aside and extensification payments be converted to it. Immediate relief may also have to be offered to small farmers in the form of income guarantees in the short term to tide them over the financial stress currently being experienced under high interest rates.

Safeguarding the countryside

The system of 'set-aside' payments, under which farmers are paid up to £80 per acre by the EC annually to take land out of production, has not helped to protect the countryside. Pressure to keep yields up is increased because of the price support system, so farmers are encouraged to farm the land left in production ever more intensively. Land that is 'set-aside' can also be under threat for change of use to intensive forestry, 'development' or golf courses.

The opposite of intensive farming is extensive farming. Extensification involves maintaining land in production, but reducing the intensity with which it is farmed and protecting wildlife habitats. It can promote diversification and regeneration of the rura economy. The EC has in the last five years started to promote extensification' by paying farmers to reduce production.

Both set-aside and extensification payments are forms of supply control, paying farmers to reduce the supply of food. 'Set-aside' payments could be effective in conjunction with other measures which ensure that land set-aside is done so for conservation reasons.

At present the government spends £10m annually on Environmentally Sensitive Areas. We propose this should be doubled initially and that suitable tracts of land (possibly redeemed from the Ministry of Defence) be identified for grants. We also propose that local authorities should have powers to make and finance Countryside Conservation Orders to protect vulnerable areas, and that the Nature Conservancy Council should be given more powers to institute Sites of Special Scientific Interest (SSSIs).

Sustainable agriculture

Under pressure from consumers, the threat of global climatic changes, and ever increasing costs, the trend away from damaging practice has already begun. The demand for organic produce - meat from naturally fed animals, and unadulterated crops - has increased awareness of the value of natural predators. Smaller acreages of mixed arable and livestock farming, with rotating crops, muck spreading and mechanical weeding, together with greater diversification including orchards, agro-forestry (to provide secondary crops of fruit, nuts and small timber), and wild areas to shelter the natural predators, can go a long way towards reducing the need for chemical fertilisers, pesticides and herbicides.

Organic farming, which avoids all chemical inputs, represents the ideal. There are already 1,000 organic farms in Britain, using under 1% of arable land. Annual sales of organic products account for only £50m out of our national food bill of £33bn. The Soil Association suggests that, with the right incentives, 20% of our 250,000 farmers could become organic by the year 2000. It needs to be noted that in the US President Bush has accepted the recommendation of the National Academy of Sciences to achieve 80% organic agriculture before the end of his term of office.

Incentives should be put in place as soon as possible. Revenues from a tax on nitrogenous fertilisers (see *Environmental taxation*) will be used to encourage conversion and to maintain income during the transition. Extension and support of the Soil Association's Symbol Scheme will be funded through grants. With a reduction in processing there would be opportunities for local marketing, and for producer co-operatives to compete effectively with the big supermarket chains.

Budget proposals

• A new EC system of environmental management payments to replace the current system of set-aside and extensification payments

• Internationally agreed cuts in CAP price subsidies to be used for environmental management payments

• Revenue from tax on nitrogenous fertilisers (up to £500m annually) to be used for short term income support and grants to encourage organic farming and the use of the Soil Association symbol

• Doubling of the money (£10m) spent on Environmentally Sensitive Areas

• Increasing the power of the Nature Conservancy Council to designate SSSIs

Impact: extra spending £0.5bn

Medium term measures

• Reorganisation of the MAFF into several ministries with clearer responsibility for food from production to consumption

• Replacement of the EC system of price subsidies by environmental management payments

• Substantial increases in the funding of the national arms of the Nature Conservancy Council

10

Housing

Over the past ten years housing problems in Britain have erupted, as witnessed most dramatically by the growing number of people sleeping rough. The government has even coined a new term, 'rooflessness'. This neatly excludes all those living in overcrowded or inadequate accommodation.

There are many other symptoms of the current housing crisis - record levels of mortgage defaults, the increasing cost of housing as a proportion of incomes, the declining number of houses available for rent and the loss in security for new tenants. Empty properties abound in the midst of housing shortage, and disrepair grows, both in urban and rural areas.

Housing is a long term issue. Today's symptoms become tomorrow's crisis, and for low income families in particular the situation is clearly worsening. We recognise that the problem is complex and multi-faceted. We need to address the root causes and seek to reverse the trend.

Broad objectives of housing policy

The basic objectives for sustainable housing policy can be expressed very straightforwardly; achieving them will be more tortuous. We suggest the following:

- decent and good quality housing for all
- affordable housing costs
- security of tenure
- flexibility to allow free movement between types of tenure and geographical areas
- involvement of occupiers permitting self-maintenance and self-build
- the highest possible environmental standards (e.g. in energy

efficiency)

Personal finance

Housing finance and taxation is possibly the most inflexible and inequitable area in society. Owner-occupiers have tax relief on their mortgage interest payments, while tenants get nothing. Since property rates were replaced by the poll tax, owners of mansions pay no more in local taxes than occupants of a bedsit. The explosion in house prices in the mid '80s was a prime factor in the growing inequity between forms of tenure, and indirectly in increasing homelessness. Until 1979 there was a system for the rationing of mortgage and other consumer credit. The Thatcher government initiated a process of financial liberalisation which had a profound impact on the housing market and the economy. Credit became far easier to obtain, not only for genuine house purchase but also for consumption via a second mortgage. The result was a boom in both house prices and in consumption (see *Monetary policy*).

We propose three measures to address these problems:

• to abolish the poll tax and introduce a land tax based on site values (see *Direct taxation*)

• to tighten the lending criteria for banks and building societies (see *Monetary policy*)

• to restrict, and eventually perhaps abolish, mortgage tax relief (see *Direct taxation*).

As a short term relief for people unable to keep up with mortgage payments we would allow 'shared-ownership'. Under this scheme the lender or another agency could take a share in the home and allow the owners to stay as tenants with a view to eventual re-purchase.

Capital finance

The recent trend has been away from subsidising new housing for rent. Dramatic reductions in home building in the public sector have contributed to the house price boom, and forced unprecedented numbers into owner-occupation. For many households, at a time of high interest rates, this has been disastrous and is reflected in record numbers of mortgage defaults.

A balanced housing policy should aim for a mix of types of tenure, and must recognise that rented housing for low earners cannot be paid for solely from rents. There will always be a need for some public subsidy. We suggest that this should be directed increasingly through non-profit agencies and the third sector (see *Informal economy*). We propose to increase the subsidy for local government and housing associations to provide affordable rented housing for low income groups, and in the first year we set aside £200m for this.

Housing has become increasingly dominated by impersonal providers - builders, local authorities. In a green society more people may wish to provide for their needs themselves, and to do so in cooperation with others. We would therefore direct support in the form of grants and loans to less orthodox forms of tenure such as housing cooperatives, and to self-build. This would be done initially via local authorities and the Housing Corporation. In the first year we would devote £50m to this.

Maintenance and repair

Disrepair is rife in UK housing. Rented accommodation is particularly bad in this respect. From this perspective the recent increase in owner-occupation may have had advantages, because such homes are more likely to be maintained, insulated and improved. However the need for government help to provide incentives is great across all sectors.

Grants to local authorities for repair of their own stock must be increased. Repair and improvement grants must be available by right to both owner-occupiers and tenants. Recent policies denying repair grants to housing associations must be reversed. Extra finance should be available to rehabilitate older housing when demolition would otherwise be the only alternative. £50m will be allocated for repair and improvement in the first year.

Other necessary measures include giving occupiers more control over repairs. The present system, which allows local authorities to carry out discretionary repairs where a private landlord defaults, must be made mandatory. Tenants in all sectors must have the right to carry out repairs in default, with bridging finance from the local authority.

Energy efficiency

Immediate measures are needed to improve energy efficiency, including a nationwide programme for home insulation. In the medium term sellers of homes should be required to provide an energy audit to the purchaser. Insulation grants must be made mandatory, and energy efficiency levels in new developments should be raised.

Housing and planning

Wider issues require that new housing should be built according to integrated planning, under which the emphasis would be accessibility as opposed to mobility. Local Structure Plans must minimise dependence on the motor car rather than cater for it.

Our proposals for *Agriculture and the countryside* reflect the need to rebuild our rural economies and re-populate our villages. In rural areas there is an acute need for affordable housing for those on low incomes. The planning laws are very restrictive, to make the conversion of agricultural or industrial land to housing very difficult. We propose that they should be relaxed in consultation with local community groups.

Homelessness

There are no simple solutions to this problem. The best long term answer would be enough housing available at affordable rents. A programme to make a start on this would be more than paid for by the savings realised from the costs of bed and breakfast accommodation. The recent trend of stripping local authorities of their housing stock can only make the situation worse. They must be permitted to switch funds from their sales of council houses and consider re-allocating bed & breakfast money towards these ends as needs become less acute.

The Homeless Persons Act must be changed to allow and encourage local authority assistance to those young single people currently excluded from it.

Community care

Despite recent legislation, community care has not become a meaningful reality for many of the elderly or disabled people who wish to remain in their own homes or their communities. DSS benefits for residential care have fallen badly behind real costs, forcing some homes to close. We propose to increase the level of benefits and the funding for domiciliary support services. In the Budget year we allocate £100m for this.

Budget proposals

- Tighten lending criteria for building societies and banks (see *Monetary policy*)
- Restrict mortgage tax relief to the basic rate (see *Direct taxation*)
- Increase subsidy to local government and housing associations for low-cost rented housing and repairs £250m
- Support for cooperative ownership and self-build
  £50m
- Permit local authorities to use funds from council house sales to build homes for rent
- Allow authorities to switch funds from B&B accommodation to construction of permanent accommodation for homeless people
- New building standards and insulation grants (see *Energy*)
- Relaxation of planning restrictions on new housing in rural areas
- Widen scope of Homeless Persons Act to include young single people
- Increased residential care benefits and domiciliary care allowances £100m

Impact: Extra spending £0.4bn

Medium term proposals

- Introduction of a land tax based on site value (see *Direct taxation*)
- Restriction of mortgage tax relief to the first ten years (see *Direct taxation*)
- Legislation to permit shared-ownership in the event of mortgage default
- Rights for tenants to do repairs in default of public landlords
- Duty on local authorities to do repairs in default of private landlords
- Further increases in support for rented housing and repairs
- Mandatory energy audit on property sales

11

Education, training and research

In spite of ever-increasing sums of money being spent, concern about the quality of education is rising. Britain is approaching a period of history when the people will need to be more skilled, educated and flexible than ever before. Ideally educational institutions should attain a workable staff-student ratio, carry out the necessary building maintenance, purchase the required equipment, offer the number of higher and further education places that the country needs, and, most importantly, open up potential in personal development for all members of society.

The last decade has been a period of intense change in both education and training. The direction of change has been to enhance the powers of the Department of Education, with a weakening of local authority control and greater self-management of schools and colleges.

Despite, or perhaps because of, these changes, there is widespread public concern about falling standards in education and a general air of crisis in schools and colleges. Teachers are aware of a decline in their status and rewards, and institutions themselves are facing recurrent funding problems. It seems that the extra resources directed into education since 1944 have given us a greater quantity, but with questionable quality.

Whereas further cuts could save the tax-payer a few p in the £, one of the oversights of government is that tax-payers are also consumers of state services and saving them money in the short term can make them worse off in the longer term. However, merely throwing money at education is unlikely to provide all the changes we need. Far too little is known about how quality is created in education. We would establish funding for research into the successes, seeking to generate a wider understanding and development of many different educational routes, and identifying a far wider variety of educational need.

Schools and colleges

The general trend over the last 30 years has been to concentrate schools into ever larger units in the name of economy. It was seen as cheaper and more effective to exploit economies of scale by closing the smaller schools and busing the children around.

Certainly a greater provision of hardware and facilities could be obtained at the new larger schools, but this was at the cost of losing so many of the intangible factors that make for good quality education. These include a sense of identity, the involvement of the community, and the human scale of the institutions.

We would seek to reverse this process by

* protecting those small schools still remaining
* encouraging and financing new small schools to opt in
* beginning the organic division of the larger units into smaller ones.

This last is the hardest, for it is always easier to destroy quality and identity than recreate it. However it is possible to direct funding to situations where previous links and present demand exist to a strong degree.

The new Education Act has introduced local management of schools and colleges (LMS and LMC), which oblige institutions to become self-managing. This has considerable merit in principle, because it lays the base for schools to become much more responsive to their own community. However there is a great danger that LMS and LMC will make the current situation considerably worse.

There is inadequate funding once local authorities relinquish control, often forcing redundancies and savage cuts in provision. Central control and direction has increased as local authority control has weakened. For example, there is the new National Curriculum to be observed for schools, and all institutions are constrained by the national pay scales. We consider that the centralising trend is not only unnecessary to ensure standards in education, but also destructive to real quality, commitment and self-reliance in our schools and colleges.

We propose to direct additional resources to making LMS and LMC work properly. In the medium term we propose a Local Education Bill to protect and enhance education on a human scale. It would enable funds to be provided for keeping existing small schools in operation and for setting up new ones. The latter may take place with the splitting up of existing large schools, when and where there is sufficient demand for it.

We would not reverse the recent weakening of local education authorities in respect of their control over individual schools and colleges. However there is still a considerable role for local education authorities, particularly in carrying out strategic functions and special needs provision over defined geographical areas. This is especially true in London, and the abolition of the ILEA was a retrograde move. We would restore the ILEA and abolish the borough education authorities.

Adult and continuing education

Education must be seen as a continuing and life-long process. This is ever more relevant now. Willingness to learn new skills will be at a premium if Britain is to adapt in a sustainable way to a rapidly changing world. Adults may be changing fields of work frequently as a matter of course, and career paths may become much less narrow and specialised.

Adult education is frequently more effective and of more lasting value than school education. The students, having enrolled voluntarily and being more mature, obtain greater benefit than teenagers who are compelled to attend school. This has been a sadly neglected sector in the past without much clout, often squeezed by the demands of school education on the one hand and higher education on the other. It is tragic that those who obtained little or no benefit from their schooldays discover motivation for learning later in life only to find that the avenues are then closed or too narrow. Our Budget would make more resources available directly to adult education and indirectly via the employment training programme.

Training and vocational qualifications

Cuts in training budgets for apprenticeships, and for higher level vocational training such as engineering degrees, have all resulted in a growing scarcity of trained and skilled workers. British businesses are now finding it increasingly difficult to recruit staff with the necessary skills and skills shortage is the dominant issue in many company boardrooms.

The recent reorganisation of employment training into 82 employer-led Technical and Enterprise Councils (TECs) is a sound idea and deserves a fair trial, despite considerable teething troubles. Unfortunately it has suffered both from over-strong central direction and from a recent cut of 30% in its £2.5bn budget - the government expecting the market to provide.

We would effectively cancel the cut and direct some of these extra resources into expanding the scope of training and vocational education. The new BTEC qualifications, equivalent to A-levels when taken to the highest levels, have been a success in a limited way in educating young people for work. Provision in the tertiary institutions must be increased. The new scheme of training credits being adopted by a number of TECs deserves to be expanded and extended. Over the medium term we would look at ways of increasing the scope to cover all unemployed people, so as to provide training at all levels, especially the middle and higher levels.

Research

At a time when concern for the environment demands that we use all our resources with maximum efficiency, UK industry is using inappropriate processes and machinery, while the government is cutting research into alternative methods.

As military (defence and defence-related) research is reduced to a level sufficient to sustain the country's conventional defensive forces, funds for civilian research must be increased. Funds must be switched to the multidisciplinary research necessary for increasing our understanding of the requirements for a sustainable society and would be channelled through new Environmental and Technology Commissions.

We regard green scientific research as a cultural activity crossing national and international boundaries. We would wish to support a wide range of individual and group projects with flexible funding, offering incentives to build on existing initiatives, with appropriate safeguards against continued bias towards high technology and job elimination operated for the benefit of big business.

Budget proposals

• Increased resources for training and technical education via training credits for school leavers and funding for TECs
£750m

• More resources to finance Local Management of Schools and Colleges and greater freedom for local setting of pay at adequate levels   £500m

• More resources for adult and continuing education
£250m

• Switching of military research spending into civilian research

Impact : spending £1.5bn

Medium term

• Restore ILEA

• Eliminate the element of compulsion in the national curriculum and the programme of national testing

• Legislation permitting freedom of curriculum for schools

• Local Education Bill protecting and promoting small secondary schools with greater involvement in the local community

• Extend training credits to cover all the unemployed population

• Grants to industry forR&D into appropriate technology for a sustainable society

• Establish Environmental and Technology Commissions to coordinate appropriate research

12

The informal economy
and the third sector

To understand an informal economy we must have some idea of
what we mean by formal. All those transactions under 'contract'
- whether buying, selling, hiring, or lending - and all those
activities where services, goods and people's time are recorded,
measured, valued and exchanged for money make up the formal
economy.

Caring in whatever form, whether within the family or within
the community - for children, for the elderly, for people with disabilities - is informal. Keeping house, digging the garden and
mowing the lawn are informal. So are working as a volunteer for
charities and political campaigning. Having parties and organ-
ising social functions are informal. The list is very long and the
amount of work is colossal, easily exceeding the whole of the
formal economy. Most of this work is still undertaken by women
and is much too important to ignore. Enabling men to make an
equal contribution to this sector (and thus release women who
prefer to work in the formal sector) is a vital factor in the need for
change (see *Direct taxation*).

There are those who seek to formalise some or all of these
activities, and give them a monetary valuation, not least so that
they could be taxed. The Wages for Housework Campaign is an
example. But the informal economy cannot be priced. How
much do you pay for neighbourly courtesy, family love? How
much money is the thought and care and organisation which
goes into a community meeting worth?

The formal/informal relationship

There is a history of encroachment of the formal economy upon
the informal. The industrialisation of the Northern nations was

a major impetus. The ideal ratio of people engaged full time in the formal economy to those in the informal supportive economy is probably about one to two. In the UK the proportion is currently almost reversed and rising.

The co-existence of formal and informal sectors is very biased. There can be no formal economy without a strong informal one. The rules of dependency appear to be:

• all participants in the formal economy are rewarded by access to its products in cash or kind

• all participants in the formal economy depend heavily on access to the products and services of the informal sector

• those whose effort is expended in the informal economy have no entitlement to products of the formal sector.

If food, accommodation and the necessities of survival are in the formal sector the fourth rule is:

• those who operate the informal economy can only survive by arranging to provide those in the formal economy with their informal needs, in a manner devised and controlled by those in the formal economy.

The health of the informal economy is under severe stress. Just as taxes are higher as a proportion of GNP than ever before, (see Figure 12.1) so the proportion of people in employment is at its highest and still increasing. When we hear that more than three million people are unemployed, we naturally think that there are fewer jobs. This is not true; there are in fact more jobs than ever, (see Figure 12.2) but even more people are seeking work in the formal economy. The question that needs to be addressed is whether this is the best use of their time, energy and human potential.

Every person who gets a job takes forty or fifty prime hours of work a week out of the informal economy. In many cases the costs themselves of taking employment almost wipe out the after-tax wage packet. Clothing, transport, baby-minders, meals out - all have to be bought out of the wage packet before there is any spare to pay the high interest rate to the bank or the mortgage which necessitated the work in the formal economy in the first place. Formal employment increases the consumption of resources - it is also stupidly inefficient.

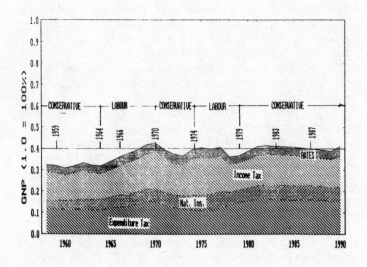

Figure 12.1 Showing tax take as a proportion of GNP

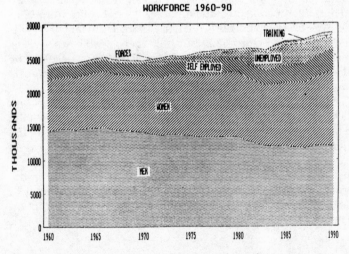

Figure 12.2 Showing increasing formal employment

The third sector

The dominant political battle of the economy in the 1970s and '80s has been between private sector and public funding. The Labour view sees the expansion of public funding as a route to more jobs and the Conservative view has been that all but the rump of public provision should be transferred to the private sector. A closer look at this oversimplified model shows that there is a significant area of activity, bridging the formal and the informal economies, which neither fulfills the profit oriented definitions of the private sector nor relies wholly on public money. This is the mysterious 'third sector'.

In the context of a post-war emergency, the socialist placing of the work formerly done by charities on a formal, publicly funded basis has been one of the great political successes of the twentieth century. The scope and volume of provision was rapidly increased, the services improved and proofed against the fluctuations in popularity which plague services reliant on gifts. The opponents of socialism are now committed to securing the same service with neither public funding nor democratic control and the voluntary sector is their chosen vehicle.

Third sector funding

In part the third sector is enabled by gifts of money and therefore does not figure as part of GNP. Gifts come from individuals and companies and many of these qualify for tax relief so that, in effect, the government subsidises them. People give their time, companies give gifts in kind and secondment of personnel, and government gives protected status through legislation.

Another source is grants and fees for service. These have increased tenfold over the last decade, fees tending to replace grants, to the point where some charities are becoming commercial organisations trading on a 'not for profit' basis.

Corporate gifts		£142m
Grants	Central Gov't	£293m
	Local Gov't	£926m
		(of which fees total £11m)
Payroll deduction		£6.5m
Personal gifts	£3bn to £4.5bn	
(Source CAF 1989*)		

Since the reporting of gifts is left to the voluntary sector itself and is restricted (by an understandable conviction that statistics are an expensive luxury) to infrequent surveys, the government's major shift in policy to regarding the voluntary sector as the heir to the responsibilities of the health and welfare services must be seen as rash in the extreme.

Care in the Community the recent White Paper (based on, but not too closely resembling, *The Griffiths Report*) setting out the programme for taking health care out of the public sector, seeks to maximise the role of charities in provision of care, although it also makes a place for private health care through insurance. This has given the go-ahead for charities to take over many of the functions of local authority service delivery and to seek permanent integration through joint capital spending programmes.

The voluntary sector in the UK is fragmented (not a fault in itself) by subject areas. For example, disability is split between the Spastics' Society, Multiple Sclerosis Society, Muscular Dystrophy Group, Chest, Heart & Stroke Association, Mencap, Mind, Royal National Institute for the Deaf, for the Blind, and so on... The population intended to benefit from these charities contains many who do not fit the definitions described, or come within the sphere serviced by a charity.

Tensions within the third sector

At its best the third sector can achieve amazing results through the amplifying effect it has on the services purchased with the money contributed. A frequently chosen mode of operation is to use the money mainly as capital to buy equipment to be used by the people who contribute their time free of charge in the informal economy. There is a tension between using donated money in this way and distributing it directly to the beneficiaries to spend for themselves, which many would prefer since this acknowledges their status as fully responsible persons in society.

There are other tensions. These include the questions of who controls policy - the givers, the recipients, or a management responsible to neither; the cost of fund raising; and the problem of paid staff. Pay in this sector has always been niggardly so that it tends to lose the best performers to better paid posts in industry and staff feel undervalued, seeing themselves as generous givers by token of the income they forego.

The green response

If we are to improve the quality of life and reduce our material consumption and the pollution it entails, we must understand that the informal economy provides essential service efficiently. Green growth lies in quality of life for every member of the ecology, not in maximising formal dealings in human commerce regardless of the cost to Earth and her many and diverse populations.

The informal sector cannot survive unless the formal sector either makes free supply of the needs of survival to all or pays adequate wages to those who work in it. It is for this reason that we regard a basic income as probably the most important mechanism whereby people can be enabled to make progress in a green society (see *Direct taxation*).

Thus the green response will be to reverse the trend to formality, to encourage a growth of the informal economy, and to ensure the health and smooth operation of this most important aspect of our lives. The green approach must be to support the informal sector by removing as far as possible the factors currently militating against it. We can then expect that it will be the growth centre of a future economy.

One of the most powerful tools for supporting the growth of the local economy will be the developing partnership between local authority, local businesses and the community. The informal economy will be at its strongest where local community projects can harness the discipline and flexibility of the private sector, and the social concern of the voluntary sector, with the accountability and the community-responsiveness of the public sector.

We therefore seek, through the basic income scheme, to extend the personal resources available to the third sector. We would also encourage radical initiatives of all sorts, not confined to the traditional causes (health, education, sport and the relief of distress), but extending into new commercial ventures, technology, research, prototype development and social initiatives.

Medium term proposals

- Implementation of a basic income scheme by 1995 (see *Direct taxation*)
- Changes in planning and building regulations to encourage home-based enterprises
- Long term reforms to income tax to encourage self-employment and part-time working (see *Direct taxation*)
- Financial help and taxation relief for childminding facilities
- Charity legislation revised to assist development of the Third Sector

13

The Local Economy

The strengthening of local economies is a vital part of building up an equitable and decentralised UK economy. Local self-reliance has been largely destroyed by the process of economic growth, yet it will become more, not less, relevant. A strong local economy is one where local communities have control over economic decisions affecting their own lives, not simply one in which there are jobs for all. This means finding ways to make better use of the resources within local communities and to encourage local production to meet local needs.

Urban development

Unemployment is largely concentrated in inner city areas. The response of both local and national government has been to entice businesses to invest in or move to these areas, with the aim of providing jobs for local people. The success of these policies is then judged according to how many jobs are created, ignoring the fact that they have been lost to another area.

Bodies such as the Urban Development Corporations have been imposed by central government, with no local public accountability. Such schemes, relying on outside support and investment leave the local economy vulnerable to decisions beyond their control; funding provided by central government can also be withdrawn by central government; large national multinational companies moving in can also move out.

This emphasis on large scale projects fails to recognise the amount of employment generated by small businesses already operating in the area. The rising value of land and therefore the price or rent of business property forces local businesses which were already in existence to close down. Large companies moving in often bring much of their skilled well paid workforce with them (incidentally also raising the price of local housing), and only leave the low paid, often part time, work for local people. The image of the unemployed and low waged as helpless victims waiting for government and industry to step in and provide for them must be changed radically to create a more enabling strategy.

Urban and rural

The interrelationship between rural and urban economies has been neglected. Rural areas are suffering from the reduction in the number of people employed in agriculture, and the resultant drift of population to cities. People looking for houses in rural areas and commuting to the city are increasing house prices out of the reach of local people. Regional economic policies need to look at both urban and rural areas together. Increasing local self reliance will require building closer links between, for instance, food growers in rural areas and the markets for that food in their local towns and cities.

Real decentralisation

Economic and political decisions are best made by the people and communities likely to be most closely affected by the consequences of those decisions. Decentralisation of power to the lowest possible level would give local people a much greater say in decisions which affect their lives. For real and workable decentralisation, there must also be a thorough-going constitutional reform of local government and the relationship with the centre (see also *Local government*). We see this as an essential precondition for supporting local economic self-reliance.

Community development

Revival and support of the local economy require policies to enable more local needs to be met by local work using local resources. Rather than encouraging existing businesses to move into a locality, leaving it vulnerable to the decisions of outsiders, industry which is owned and controlled by local people must be both expanded and initiated. Structures such as workers' cooperatives which give greater control over companies to those working in them should be encouraged.

Community involvement at every stage of a development programme designed to use the resources of local people is an essential prerequisite. Democratically and locally controlled bodies must be set up:

• to enable a wide range of people from the community to participate in the development of policy, strategy, projects and enterprises

• to give local businesses advice and assistance in finding finance

• to increase cooperation between local businesses through local purchasing networks

• to provide a forum for partnership between local authority, local businesses and the community (see *The informal economy*).

• to produce local audits to show areas (such as energy) where a local community was dependent, perhaps entirely, on materials or services produced in other regions. Strategies to provide these more locally must then be developed in cooperation with local people.

Health care in the community

Good health is a primary human resource and its conservation comes high on the list of green priorities. The pace and rate of change of life in our society generate threats to physical and mental health faster than our natural defences can respond and we either accept increasing numbers of casualties of progress or improve our social mechanisms for anticipating, detecting and controlling hazards.

In the long term green economic policies aim to achieve a 'health dividend' like the 'peace dividend' measured not only in money but in reduction of risk and human suffering. We would shift the emphasis immediately from preparing to attack disease to removing threat, and improving what defence is unavoidable.

Our commitment includes a vital ingredient - the continuing availability of competent advice, care and support for all who seek it. Given professional advice at the appropriate level, self-help groups in the community can undertake considerable responsibility. For example, tranquiliser withdrawal groups supported by both social and health workers can not only reduce addiction, and enhance quality of life, but also significantly reduce costs.

This assistance extends beyond the afflicted person to their family, friends, partners, employers - the community whose lives are touched by the problem and whose understanding and support make the difference between rejection and dependency and the fullest possible social integration.

The local economy must eventually be strong enough to make a direct contribution to local community health care (as well as indirectly) but most importantly, through the improvement to the local environment.

The role of councils

There is much which local councils can do to encourage local self reliance. As well as investing local government revenue in building the local economy, councils can use their purchasing policies to buy from local industry. Restrictions when putting council work out to private tender must be removed, so that use of local workforce, etc. can be specified. Councils can also make more use of their pension funds, diversifying their portfolios to the benefit of the local area.

Community banking

The existing financial system allows the concentration of economic power into a few institutions. Money has been allowed to flow freely in search of the greatest return. If the size of the financial return on an investment is all-important, then wider social and environmental questions are ignored.

There is therefore need for far greater local self-reliance in finance. Money should be kept as far as possible within local communities rather than being siphoned off by banks for more profitable investment elsewhere. The establishment of local community banks and regional investment banks (see *Monetary policy*) would enable people's savings to be invested to help their own communities. Community banks would have a much greater degree of accountability to local people than the commercial banks. They would often be prepared to lend in areas considered too high a risk by conventional banks, usually those areas most in need of investment. Other initiatives such as credit unions and local currencies, which put monetary control directly in the hands of local people would also be encouraged.

Medium term proposals

• constitutional reform along decentralist lines (see *Local government*)

• promotion of partnership bodies to carry out social and environmental audits and to devise local economic development strategies

• development of local economic indicators for use in pollution control and economic development (see *Environmental taxation*)

• drafting of sustainable economic development plans for regions and districts

• the establishment of a network of community, municipal and regional banks (see *Monetary policy*)

• support for credit unions, skills barter schemes

• investigation of local currencies

14

Local Government

Local government has tremendous potential both in 'greening' the economy and encouraging devolution of power to communities. Unhappily successive national governments have treated local government almost as a plaything of Whitehall. Our Budget would start to reverse that process.

Of all industrialised countries, Britain has one of the most centralised systems of government and public finance. Local authorities are historically and constitutionally subordinate to Parliament, both in duties and revenue-raising powers.

In population terms, other countries' municipalities are more like our parishes and the UK districts are equivalent to counties and provinces elsewhere. In some countries municipalities of just a few thousand people are allowed to take on a whole range of functions and can choose to federate to do so more effectively.

From the end of the Second World War until the 1970s local government became increasingly the agent of the national government, particularly in respect of implementing the welfare state. The relationship was on a fairly amicable basis, eased by continuing increases in real local spending and generous rate-support grants from national government. Since then government concern over the level of public spending has made the relationship increasingly antagonistic, culminating in ministers and civil servants taking the power to dictate the limits of local spending. Whitehall now determines the level of revenue support grant and can decide whether to cap locally-raised tax.

Local taxes

This recent trend results in greater regulation of which services and duties local authorities should perform; tighter control of how much they can spend; and a smaller proportion of spending raised by locally set taxes.

The Uniform Business Rate (UBR) replaced business rates previously set locally with a national rate based on revalued property values. The UBR has provoked widespread anxiety in small retail businesses, particularly in the South and West, who face very large increases in rate over the five year phasing-in period. According to a survey by the Forum of Private Business in 1990, up to 45,000 businesses faced closure (reported in *The Times*, 25 April 1990) and the prospects for 1991 are worse. The burden is of course compounded for those retailers living 'over the shop', who now pay the poll tax in addition to the business rate.

The community charge, or poll tax, has been almost universally unpopular and for good reason. It violates every canon of taxation, being expensive and difficult to collect, not too hard to evade, hedged around with numerous reliefs and safety nets, and unrelated to ability to pay. There was a concern about accountability of local councils under rates, and the community charge was supposed to overcome this. That was soon seen as a mirage, given the small proportion of local government income that poll tax covers and the widespread recognition of it as a tax imposed by central government. The poll tax should be abolished, and the sooner the better. However it is less easy to say what should take its place.

Alternatives to the present system

The previous system was coming under increasing pressure and reform was widely felt to be necessary. If the wider questions are considered there are really only two consistent routes to reform. One is to continue the trend and recognise the reality of local government as agent of national government, thus destroying the last vestiges of accountability. Local spending would be financed 100% by the centre, and there could be savings in local administration. The other is to enact constitutional reforms in a decentralist or federal direction. This would give increased responsibilities to local authorities and allow them the right to raise revenue to carry them out.

The main difference from the present system would be the right of authorities to determine their own spending levels. The first route attempts to provide equality and uniformity of service provision via central control, while the second offers local democracy and accountability, along with greater diversity and self-reliance, via decentralist reform.

Our clear preference is for constitutional reform for local government along decentralist lines. Constitutional reform is vital, because to merely hand over functions to many of the existing authorities, with their currently defined areas, would be self-defeating. Such reform should in the long run comprise:

• regional (in England), Scottish and Welsh tiers of government

• devolution of functions from Whitehall to lower tiers

• devolution of functions from existing local authorities to new community councils or parish councils

• electoral reform and greater accountability of councillors

Each tier of government would have tax-raising powers.

Local government has been subjected to unprecedented re-organisation over recent years, and the system is in great need of some time to settle down. Nonetheless it would be dangerous and possibly self-defeating to attempt devolution of finance without the necessary accompanying constitutional changes.

We therefore propose that a start on constitutional changes should be made at the same time as changes to local government finance. We propose taxation and financial reforms which in the first year deal with the worst excesses of the poll tax, and we would phase in constitutional reform over the medium term.

Changes in the first year

One year is inadequate to introduce new alternatives to the poll tax or to re-introduce rates. However our view is it is best to abolish the poll tax immediately rather than try to keep it going for even one year while preparing for alternatives. There would be great savings in the time and effort of town hall staff. It would provide a breathing space and a chance to dissipate some of the ill will that has built up between the government, councils and their electorate. But perhaps most importantly, it would dramatically relieve the burden on the people most affected by the tax, those families with incomes not low enough to qualify for rebates.

The revenue estimated from the poll tax in one year is £10-12bn. This could be raised by, for instance, either a 6p or 7p rise in the basic rate of income tax and perhaps more on higher rates, or an increase in the standard rate of VAT to 20%.

Each proposal has its problems. Raising the basic rate of income tax to 40p (25p + 9p + 6p see *Direct taxation*) would worsen the employment trap and perhaps also increase tax evasion. Raising VAT by 5% would be a regressive move. However either would be infinitely preferable to muddling along with the poll tax. We propose the use of income tax. This amounts to a 'local income tax' supplement of 6p in the basic rate, and would last for one year only.

Local taxation options

The Layfield Report on Local Government Finance recommended in 1975 that local income tax (LIT) presented the best single alternative to domestic rates. This is an attractive option now that the computerisation of the Inland Revenue makes it feasible at low additional cost.[30] We propose that LIT should be one of the options available for local authorities to choose from.

The introduction of taxation based on imputed rent from site values makes good economic and environmental sense (*see Direct taxation*), and has been most recently proposed by Muellbauer in a 1990 study for the Institute for Public Policy Research.[35] A national component of a site value tax levied on residential land could be integrated with the national income tax. It could also form part of a LIT component for local taxation. There could be both locally-set and nationally-set components.

One improvement in business rates is to limit these only to site values rather than business values. We support this, and propose that the Uniform Business Rate as such be retained only until authorities have available their preferred mix of local taxation.

The next alternative is the return of local property rates, both for business and for residences. Although taxation based on property values has its disadvantages, such as the discouragement of improvement and the adverse effect on local business, our view is that councils should be able to use it if they wish.

Reforms for the medium term

We suggest that the following principles should be established in local government finance in the medium term:
* taxes under local control must be increased back to the

levels prevailing before introduction of the poll tax and UBR, and then increased still further. A upper limit will be reached because of the need to redistribute funds between areas of different wealth, but a figure of 70% of necessary revenue to be raised locally should be attainable, with commensurate reduction in central taxation

• local authorities should have a choice of a mix of taxation and monetary instruments, and a return of their powers to raise taxes from business. This will give councils greater leverage over the local economy and also strengthen local democracy. This choice will improve the situation which arose under business rates, when poorer areas set higher rates where property values were low and the needs of the population were greatest. The result was often a spiral of economic decline.

• taxation should be based on ability to pay and be hard to shift or evade, easy to understand and naturally buoyant

• there should be scope for environmental taxation at the local level.

Local authority debt

We see the continuation of high levels of local authority debt as an unnecessary millstone. Rather than have to go to the money markets for capital finance, local authorities could be financed from their own municipal banking system (see *Monetary policy*), or in some cases issuing bonds to their local citizens.

Debt owed to the banking system could be eliminated over a number of years by the issue of special non-interest bearing bonds by the Bank of England on behalf of the Treasury. A phased programme whereby central government writes off a proportion each year by the debt-free issue of new money could also be considered. A limited amount of new money could be raised by issuing local authority bonds (i.e. borrowing from the local public as was common in the '50s and '60s).

Redistribution of taxation revenues

It will always be essential for there to be some redistribution of taxation revenues from richer to poorer regions, in order to maintain mandatory minimum standards of service provision. We recognise that there is a tension between equity on the one hand and local democracy and accountability on the other. The rate support grant formula was an attempt to redistribute wealth between regions, but it was under the control of the centre. The grant system has become a weapon in the hands of the Government to make local authorities spend less.

A new constitutional agreement could allow for more regional diversity (for instance in education or health care), while encouraging much greater autonomy in the planning and running of key services like energy and transport. We propose that an Association of Local Authorities (combining existing bodies) be set up which will convene a Local Government Forum to discuss the options for decentralisation and redistribution.

For the long term we see no alternative to establishing a formula to handle redistribution of revenues. However it should be simpler and more independent of the centre. One method is to use as the fund for redistribution an agreed proportion of the revenue from a central tax which is levied according to ability to pay. Income tax (or just the site value component of it) could well be used, together with a uniform component of business rates. The revenue from the chosen tax(es) is put into a central pool and redistributed according to a formula based on population and other factors, in a manner similar to the current method. In this way the overall size of the 'cake' to be distributed to local authorities is less subject to political manoeuvre.

Budget proposals

• Poll tax would be abolished immediately. (The poll tax registers would be maintained for possible use in the payment of a basic income.)

• Revenue Support Grants to local authorities would be increased. Grant for the first year would therefore cover the whole of expected local government expenditure

• A system of independent tribunals would be set up to administer requests from councils for more grant

• Uniform Business Rate would be retained for one year

Medium-term proposals

• A nationwide tax on site values, applying to both residential land and land used for business purposes (including agriculture)

• National site value tax on residential land to be integrated with national income tax

• Options for locally-set precepts on site value (business and residential land) and on property value (residential land only)

• Domestic rates to be reactivated on the basis of the old valuation and available to councils

• Uniform business rate to be replaced by local site value tax

• Local authorities empowered to set LIT, site value tax, and property rates levels. The target is 50% of spending needs to be met by local taxes in that year, rising to 70% within four years, with commensurate reduction in central taxation

• Options for local authorities to introduce particular forms of expenditure tax, such as local sales taxes

• A local government forum to be convened to examine, among other things, alternative ways of supplementing local taxation revenue with distribution from a central pool

• Decentralist constitutional reform

15

Europe, world trade
and global security

More than ever before, the UK economy is influenced by complex and sometimes conflicting economic trends in the rest of the world. Recent events in Eastern Europe suggest we may have to re-think 'Europe' altogether. If the other '1992' (the international convention on greenhouse gas emissions to be signed at the UN Conference on Sustainable Development in Brazil in 1992) is to be successful, rich and poor nations will have to agree economic policies very different from those which dominate domestic and world economies today.

In this chapter we look briefly at some of the main trends which most influence the UK economy.

The European Economic Community
The 1957 Treaty of Rome (supposedly to be accomplished by 1969) boiled down to a single objective - to create a barrier-free internal market by abolishing 'obstacles to freedom of movement for persons, services and capital'. The 1987 Single European Act (SEA) had a double objective: the completion of the internal market by 1992 (23 years late!), and a united European response to the intensification of economic competition from the United States and Japan.[16]

There are powerful contradictions between the sort of policies which will create an internal market offering reasonably equal benefits to all its members and the sort of policies which will render the EC a lean and mean competitor in the world marketplace. The evidence suggests that, in tune with the experience of the globalising economy so far, the competitive policies are winning.

We believe that these internal strains will doom the 1992

bject to failure. The consequences of that failure will continue to be borne mostly by the environment and nations on the periphery of the EC.[17] Whether the periphery is defined in economic, political, environmental or geographical terms, the UK falls into this category on several counts.

The pressure for economic and monetary union (EMU) came from pressure from the Commission bureaucracy. UK entry in the ERM put one more stepping stone into place for the Delors plan. However the UK attitude to EMU is lukewarm at the most, and the move was clearly made for domestic reasons (permitting a modest cut in interest rates). We argue (see *Monetary policy*) that UK membership of the ERM can be accepted for the short term, but that EMU should be opposed because of the threat it poses to regional and local autonomy.

In the short term, we seek constructive reform from within the EC (particularly of the CAP - see *Agriculture*), but our medium term strategy is for a strong all-European regional policy. This combines large-scale cooperation on areas like global warming and other (newly defined) security matters with smaller scale cooperation to establish ecologically sustainable local economies.

The broader Europe

In an increasingly unstable world economy, the European Free Trade Area nations (Sweden, Norway, Finland, Iceland, Switzerland and Austria) are varyingly aware of the danger of staying aloof from, or merely having a special relationship with, the consolidating European economic bloc.

The revolution in Eastern Europe, particularly the unification of Germany, is bound to affect the economic balance within the EEC and its external economic relationships. Many members of governments in Eastern Europe are far from convinced that the economic medicine prescribed by the West will work, but are obliged to swallow it in return for much needed emergency aid. Quite aware that the EC doesn't want any more weak members and that its member states are very nervous about an influx of economic and environmental refugees from the East, Eastern European countries are nevertheless likely to seek access to the 'European economic space' to press the rest of Europe to take their preferred framework for a new Europe more seriously.

Finance, aid and trade

East Europeans are right to look askance at proposals to establish a European Bank for Reconstruction and Development). Modelled on the World Bank, it could well be instrumental, as the World Bank was in the Third World, in siphoning cash and resources out of eastern Europe instead of getting them to where they are needed most.

There is already considerable and mounting evidence that the global banking and financial system has not been operating in the interests either of society or the environment. The total of international debt exceeds $1000bn and every year there is a net transfer of wealth from the poorer to the richer nations. Debt and interest payments in 1988 cost Africa, Asia and Latin America $178bn - three times as much as the aid they received (Figure 15.1).

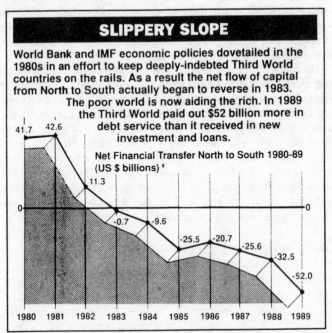

Reproduced courtesy of the New Internationalist (Dec 1990)

Debtor countries have been compelled to adopt economic policies which hurt the poorest most. Furthermore there is now overwhelming evidence that many of the original loans (mostly from private banks) which inaugurated Third World debt were for projects which were uneconomic even in conventional terms, and which were disastrous for the environment.

The role of the International Monetary Fund (IMF) and the World Bank has been almost completely destructive both to the environment and economic security in the Third World. It is conceivable, but unlikely, that they could be reformed to promote sustainability and equity. However the need for radical reform goes beyond multilateral institutions to embrace the whole financial system.

In the long term money should revert to its original role as a means of exchange to facilitate trade, rather than a means of control. Global consensus among rich nations to achieve this is highly unlikely until there is a debt-triggered collapse in the world economy. In the meantime we propose that the UK and like-minded countries should work to develop self-reliance and independence from global financial markets - an extremely difficult but not impossible task.

Theoretically, trading relationships should be voluntary and both partners should gain from the exchange. However, the latest round of negotiations under General Agreement on Tariffs and Trade (GATT) make abundantly clear that this is far from being the case in practice. Prices are set not only by supply and demand, but by relative power.[53] The fallacy of free trade is of course linked to the fallacy of the perfect market. While local markets may be able to assemble the essential ingredients of a fair and free transaction, global markets most assuredly cannot. In the long term a green GATT seems the only way to harmonise trade with the needs for ecological sustainability and equity.

Towards global environmental security

At the same time as peace was breaking out over Europe, the extent of environmental degradation was becoming clearer. Pictures of toxic waste dumps and belching brown coal-fired power stations poured out of eastern Europe, while climate scientists pored over graphs of soaring greenhouse gas emissions. Calculations of the consequences of unecological economic policies to human and environmental health are now being be made on a global scale.

The spectre of millions of people on the move, whether escaping from poisoned soils, the infertile dust of expanding deserts, shrinking water tables or rising sea levels, brings with it the imperative to redefine human security. More and more, people are starting to recognise that national security may in future be measured not in battalions of soldiers but in numbers of people happy to stay at home.

The people of Europe face a clear choice. This is between continuing to sacrifice the environment and more and more people to the demands of the economy, and seeking real wealth and security. For Russia in particular, the 35-nation Conference for Security and Cooperation (CSCE) in Europe provides a much more attractive neutral territory on which East and West Europeans could meet to discuss new institutions for economic, environmental and security cooperation.

As the failure of the globalising economy to provide for local needs increases, the sort of protectionism and bartering which will inevitably follow can be viewed as a positive trend towards more regional economic self-reliance. The thrust of our medium-term policies is based on the notion that healthy national self-reliance provides the basis for trade relationships founded on cooperation not competition (i.e. genuinely free and of mutual benefit).[14]

Global security

'As a ruined country we shall have no need of defence. An impoverished people have no need for an army,' is how Russian Foreign Secretary Eduard Shevardnadze completed the epitaph of the Warsaw Pact.[46] In the West, the prospect of a 'peace dividend' lit up the eyes of Financial Ministers struggling and increasingly failing to make the ends of national budgets meet.

The potential to redirect the cash spent on military definitions of security into environmental definitions of security is immense. World-wide, military expenditure runs at about $1,000bn, roughly 10% of all world economic activity and approximately the same as the total Third World debt. The world's annual $100bn military research and development budget is actually greater than all government research expenditure on developing new technologies, improving human health, increasing agricultural productivity and reducing birth-rates.[43]

We propose to release significant funds over the next few years from conventional defence expenditures in the UK (*see Defence*). Conversion of the expertise and plant of the defence industry to develop and commercialise tele-communications, renewable energy technologies and other energy efficient technologies, will be complemented by funds which will go directly to helping Third World and eastern European countries leap-frog into low energy-use economic strategies.

Budget proposals

• Opposition to Economic and Monetary Union in the European Community
• An additional £500m in total to Eastern Europe and the Third World towards emergency know-how transfer to aid environmental regeneration and the development of self-reliant local economies
• De-linking of all aid (bi-lateral and multi-lateral) from trade agreements
• Aid to be targetted on schemes to restore ecological sustainability and promote equity and decentralisation
• A set of ethics to be drawn up and published to govern all international relationships
Impact: cost £0.5 billion

Medium term proposals

• Conversion of defence industries to peaceful uses
• Promote a Europe of self-reliant regions through a transformed EEC or through the Council of Europe or the CSCE working in the framework of a reformed United Nations
• Further reform to the CAP
• Promote regionalisation of world commodity markets, with bi-lateral and multi-lateral trading agreements based on sustainability and equity (a green GATT).
• Work towards independence from international financial markets and global financial reform

16

Budget Summary and Balance

Summary of budget proposals

The Green Budget is a self-financing package of emergency measures that can be taken immediately by a British government. Policies for the medium term are also put forward in each policy area.

The Budget strategy is threefold:

1. To start to build an ecologically sustainable economy, via environmental taxation amd recycling of half the revenues into the 'supply-side'.

2. To attack the poverty trap with large increases in child benefit and the basic tax allowance. The medium term objective is an unconditional basic income of £35 per week paid to all adults.

3. To begin a process of decentralisation in the economy, with the poll tax and Uniform Business Rate replaced by locally-decided and locally-set taxation.

The proposals are estimated to raise about £8 billion in extra revenue (after indexing tobacco, alcohol and petrol duties for inflation). Half of the extra revenue is spent on 'supply-side' measures in areas like energy conservation, and about half is spent on a large increase in child benefit and 5% increases in income support and pensions.

Direct taxation
• Increase in the basic personal allowance by 50% to £4500 pa
• Consolidation of employees' National Insurance into basic rate of income tax
• Cut of 1p in the basic rate, making a new rate of 33p in the £
• Change of income tax from taxable income system to 'zero rate' system
• Increase the higher rate of income tax to 50p, starting at £30,000 pa
• An intermediate rate of 44p, starting at £24,000 pa
• Restriction of mortgage tax relief to the basic rate and first ten years
• Tax-free interest deposits in community/regional banks and 'local equity'
• Introduction of site value tax within three years

Benefits
• Increase in child benefit by 50%
• Increase in pensions and benefits to compensate for indirect tax increases
• Rescindment of 1988 changes to income support rules affecting homeless and young people
• Introduction of an unconditional basic income of £35 per week by 1995

Environmental taxation
• A carbon tax on all fossil fuels at an initial average rate of 8%
• Introduction of a nitrate tax on fertilisers of 40%
• Introduction of pollution taxation
* Increase in petrol and diesel duty by 75p per gallon

Other taxation
• A local income tax supplement to the basic rate of income tax of 6p for one year only (to pay for abolition of the poll tax)
• Imposition of VAT on all domestic fuels
• Zero-rating for VAT of all goods carrying the new 'environmental label'
• Increase of tobacco duty by 21%
• Increase of beer, wine and spirits duties by 15%

Monetary policy
- Controls on lending by banks and building societies
- Personal credit controls legislation
- New community banks and regional investment banks
- Managed devaluation within the Exchange Rate Mechanism
- Opposition to Economic and Monetary Union

Supply areas
- Cut in defence spending of £0.5 billion
- Additional aid to Europe and the Third World of £0.5 billion
- A nationwide programme of energy conservation of £1bn pa
- Programme of investment in windpower and CHP of £1bn pa
- Cancellation of the £17bn roads programme and redirection into public transport
- An extra £1.5bn for education and training, concentrating on local management of schools, adult education and training credits for all school-leavers
- A redirection of agricultural grants from price support towards environmental management
- Immediate £0.5bn for farm income support and organic farming

Local government
- Immediate abolition of poll tax, to be replaced for one year by equivalent grants from central government (funded by temporary supplement to income tax)
- Preparation for local income tax and the reactivation of property rates to be available for local authorities from in the second year
- Site value tax to provide an additional source of revenue in the third year
- Retention of Uniform Business Rate until replaced by site value tax
- Accompanying programme of decentralist constitutional reform

Other measures
- Support for local economic development agencies
- Preparation of local environmental audits and local targets for environmental indicators

Balance sheet

Estimated changes in revenue from the Green Budget proposals.
Figures for indirect taxation are those calculated after indexing
for inflation where appropriate.

Changes in taxation

Positive numbers indicate tax increases,
negative numbers indicate tax cuts.
Where appropriate, figures are calculated after indexation.

	(£ billion)
Direct taxation	-1.9
Carbon tax	1.8
Nitrogenous fertiliser tax	0.1
Increase in petrol and diesel duty	5.2
Increase in tobacco and alcohol duties	0.8
Abolition of tax reliefs on company cars	0.7
VAT on domestic energy supply	1.7
Poll tax abolition	-10.0
Poll tax income tax supplement	10.0
Total extra revenue	**8.4**

Changes in benefits

Positive figures mean increases in spending

Increase in child benefit of 50%	2.3
Increase in income support rates by 5%	1.1
Increase in retirement pension by 5%	0.5

Total extra spending   3.8

Changes in spending

Defence (net)	-0.5
Aid to Europe and Third World	0.5
Energy	2.0
Transport (net)	0.0
Agriculture	0.5
Housing	0.4
Education, training and research	1.5

Total extra spending   4.4

Overall balance   +0.2

Positive figure indicates surplus

Notes

1. The effects of income tax changes were estimated using a small model of the tax system and Inland Revenue data.

2. All other changes were modelled using a simple spreadsheet model with latest available government information.

3. Revenue from indirect taxation and transport taxation is that extra revenue over and above indexing duties for inflation (estimated at 10% pa).

4. Any small discrepancies between individual items and column totals arise from rounding.

BIBLIOGRAPHY AND REFERENCES

1.   Anderson, V., *Alternative Economic Indicators*, London, Routledge, 1991.

2.   *Agriculture in the United Kingdom*, MAFF, HMSO, 1989

3.   Barker, T., Dunne, P. and Smith, R., *Measuring the Peace Dividend in the United Kingdom*, supplement to *Industry and the British Economy*, Cambridge Econometrics. (Also forthcoming in Journal of Peace Research), 1990.

4.   Barker, T. and Cope, D., (eds), *Green Futures for Economic Growth: Britain in 2010*, Cambridge Econometrics, 1991

5.   Barrett, S., *Pricing the Environment: the Economic and Environmental Consequences of a Carbon Tax*, Centre for Economic Forecasting Economic Outlook, Vol. 14 No. 5, London Business School, 1990.

6.   Bowers, J., *Economics of the Environment: the Conservationists' Response to the Pearce Report*, Telford, British Association of Nature Conservationists, 1990.

7.   Chalmers, M., *UK Defence Requirements 1990-2000*, Saferworld, London, 1989.

8.   *Charity Trends*, Charities Aid Foundation (CAF) 12th ed, 1989

9.   Cobb, J. and Daly, H., *For the Common Good*, U.S.A., Beacon Press, and London, Greenprint, 1990.

10.   Council for the Preservation of Rural England, *Roads to Ruin*, London, 1990.

11.   Dauncey, G., *After the Crash: the Emergence of the Rainbow Economy*, Greenprint, 1988.

12.   U.K. Department of Energy, *The Demand for Energy*, in *The Market for Energy*, D. Helm, J. Kay and D. Thompson (eds.), Oxford, Oxford University Press, 1989.

13.   Ekins, P., *The Living Economy: a New Economics in the Making*, London, Routledge and Kegan Paul, 1986.

14.   Ekins, P., *Trade for Mutual Self-Reliance*, paper for The Other Economic Summit, London, May 1989

15.   Etzone A., *The Moral Dimension: Towards a New Economics*, Free Press, New York, 1988

16.   European Commission, *Europe without Frontiers - Completing the Internal Market*, European Documentation Series No 3, 1988

17.   European Commission, *Task Force Report on the Environment and the Internal Market, '1992': The Environmental Dimension*, 1990,

18.   Fickett, A.P. , Gellings, C.W., and Lovins, A.B., *Efficient Uses of Electricity*, Scientific American, November 1990.

19.   Goldsmith, E., Bunyard, P. and Hildyard, N., *The Social and Environmental Effects of Large Dams*, Wadebridge Ecological Centre, 1984.

20.   Personal communication

21.   Gray, R.H., *The Greening Of Accountancy: the Profession after Pearce*, London, Report for the Chartered Association of Certified Accountants, Certified Accountants Publications Ltd, 1990.

22.   Green Party, *Manifesto for a Sustainable Society*, The Green Party, London, 1990.

23.   Helm, D., and Pearce, D. (eds), *Economic Policy towards the Environment*, Oxford Review of Economic Policy, Vol. 6 No. 1., Oxford University Press, 1990.

24.   International Monetary Fund, *Finance and Development*, March 1989, IMF Washington, DC

25.   Institute for Public Policy Research, *Takeover and Short-termism*, London, IPPR, 1990.

26.   Intergovernmental Panel on Climate Change, *Reports from Working Groups I, II and III*, World Meteorological Organisation and UN Environmental Programme, Geneva, 1990.

27.   Jacobs, M., *The Green Economy*, London, Greenprint (The Merlin Press), 1990.

28.   Jackson, T., and Roberts, S., *Getting out of the Greenhouse: An Agenda for Action on Energy Policy*, Friends of the Earth, London, 1989.

29.   Jenkins, T.N., *Future Harvests: The Economics of Farming and the Environment: Proposals for Action*, Report to the Council for the Preservation of Rural England and the WWF(UK), CPRE, 1990.

30.   Kay, J., and Smith, S., Local Income Tax, Options for the Introduction of the Local Income Tax in the UK, Institute of Fiscal Studies, Report 31, London, 1988.

31.   Lean, G., et al, *Atlas of the Environment*, Arrow Books Ltd, London, 1990.

32.   Legget, J. (ed.), *Global Warming: The Greenpeace Report*, Oxford University Press, 1990.

33.   Mayer, C., and Alexander, I., *Banks and Securities Markets: Corporate Financing in Germany and the UK*, London, CEPR Discussion Paper 443, 1990.

34.   Miles, D., *Financial Liberalisation, The Housing Market and the Current Account*, Birkbeck College, London, 1990.

35.   Muellbauer, J., *The Great British Housing Disaster and Economic Policy*, London, Institute for Public Policy Research, Economic Study No. 5, 1990.

36.   National Right to Fuel and Neighbourhood Energy Action, *Fuel Poverty and the Greenhouse Effect*, Newcastle, Neighbourhood Energy Action, 1990.

37.   Netherlands, Ministry of Housing, Planning and the Environment, *National Environmental Policy Plan* (and update *NEPP Plus*), The Hague, 1989 (and 1990).

39.   OECD, *The Polluter Pays Principle: Definition, Analysis, Implementation*, Paris, OECD, 1975.

40.   Parker, H., *Instead of the Dole: An Enquiry into the Integration of the Tax and Benefit Systems*, London and New York, Routledge, 1989.

41.   Pearce, D., Markandya, A. and Barbier, E., *Blueprint For A Green Economy*, London, Earthscan Publications Ltd, 1989.

42.   Pearson, M., and Smith, S., *Taxation and Environmental Policy: Some Initial Evidence*, Institute for Fiscal Studies Commentary No. 19. 1990

43.   Renner, M., *National Security: The Economic and Environmental Dimensions*, Worldwatch Paper 89, May 1989, Worldwatch Insitute, Washington DC.

44.   Robertson, J., *Future Wealth*, London, Mansell Publishing, 1989.

45.   Robins, N., *Is 1992 Sustainable? A New Economics Response*, paper for the Institute for European Environmental Policy Seminar: 1992 and the Environment, March 1990

46.   Shevardnadze, E., S*peech to 28th Party Congress*, July 1990

47.   Shields, J., *Controlling Household Credit*, National Institute Economic Review, August 1988, pp 46-55.

48.   Southwood, P., *The Peace Dividend in the 1990s*, London, Campaign for Nuclear Disarmament, 1990.

49.   *Statement on the Defence Estimates 1990*, Ministry of Defence, HMSO, 1990.

50.   *Statement on the 1990 Community Budget*, CM1059, HMSO, April 1990.

51.   Stockholm Environmental Institute, *Responding to Climate Change: Tools for Policy Development*, Stockholm, 1990.

52.   Taverne, R., *Institute of Economic Affairs Review*, 1990, Vol. 11 No. 1.

53.   UNICEF, *The State of the World's Children*, 1990, UNICEF, New York.

54.   *Warm Homes - Cool Planet*, published jointly by Right to Fuel, Neighbourhood Energy Action, Heatwise Glasgow and Friends of the Earth, 1990.

55.   Weinberg, C. J., and Williams, R. H., *Energy from the Sun*, in Scientific American, September 1990.

56.   World Commission on Environment and Development (Brundtland Commision), *Our Common Future*, Oxford University Press, 1987.

57.   Worldwatch Institute, *State Of The World 1990*, W.W. Norton, New York and London.